Richard Wilbur
A Bibliographical Checklist

Richard Wilbur

A Bibliographical Checklist

by John P. Field
West Chester State College

With a note by
Richard Wilbur

The Kent State University Press

The Serif Series

Bibliographies and Checklists, Number 16

William White, General Editor
Wayne State University

With thanks to Hugh Staples

So long as he is capable of doing new work, a writer keeps putting his old work behind him. Some of it he forgets entirely, and he mutes his memory of the rest, so as to avoid any relaxing sense of accomplishment. It would have been a doubtful practice for me to record the facts which Mr. John Field has here compiled with such patience, accuracy, and logic. I thank him for an excellent job, and I am grateful for his implicit judgment that my work was worthy of his trouble.

—RICHARD WILBUR

Contents

Introductory Note

Richard Wilbur was born March 1, 1921, in New York City.
He graduated from Amherst College in 1942, served with
the U. S. Army in Europe during the Second World War, and
has taught English at Harvard, Wellesley, and Wesleyan—
where he is currently Professor of English.

Wilbur's career as a writer has now spanned almost thirty
years. Best known as a poet, he is also a distinguished translator,
was the principal lyricist for the musical version of Voltaire's
Candide, and has produced an impressive body of literary
criticism and editorial work. His poetic canon alone includes
five volumes of verse as well as numerous uncollected pieces.
Although by all standards a successful poet—Wilbur has,
for instance, received both the Pulitzer Prize for Poetry and the
National Book Award, as well as many other honors—his
achievement has also been passed off frequently as a matter of
technical brilliance coupled with thematic insignificance.
And, while a great deal has been written about Wilbur's work,
much of it has stemmed from the "war" between those who
stand for a return to formalism in contemporary American
poetry and those who represent reaction against traditional
forms: Wilbur has been identified as a leader of the traditional,
or academic, school, and either attacked or defended as such.
Despite the controversy about his achievement, however, there
seems little doubt that Wilbur has produced an important

body of poetry which has earned him a place among the most significant poets of his time.

Wilbur's position in American letters is certainly such that a bibliographical record of the large amount of material written by and about him seems in order. Almost nothing along these lines has yet been done, however. A very useful list was included by Donald Hill in his recent volume about Wilbur (*see below*, Section II, A), but it is quite brief and highly selective. The following bibliographical checklist is intended to be comprehensive. It has a two-fold purpose: to provide a chronological ordering of approximately the first thirty years of Wilbur's activity as a writer, and to furnish an aid that will facilitate a fuller understanding of his intention and technique. It also includes a listing of the criticism of his work published in America and England and a few items from other countries— mainly France. A full survey of the translations of poems and the critical studies in foreign languages has not proved feasible at the present time, however. In addition to the chron-ological record, I have indicated the different versions of the individual poems, although most of Wilbur's revisions after publication are relatively minor in nature, and a comparison of variants is usually not of much help in understanding either his meaning or his method. The list of individual poems includes a sizeable number that have not been collected in any of Wilbur's five published volumes of verse.

I have personally checked all but a small fraction of the information supplied in this checklist. The unverified entries that I have listed below were all found in several sources or in single sources that seemed very reliable. In a few cases I have included incomplete citations when there seemed no doubt about their authenticity, on the assumption that a good clue is better than no information at all; this situation is most noticeable in the Book Reviews section (II, C).

J. P. F.

West Chester, Pennsylvania

I. Works by Richard Wilbur

A. Books

1. Volumes of poetry

Listed chronologically.

The Beautiful Changes and Other Poems. New York: Reynal & Hitchcock, 1947. 55 pages. Subsequent printings identified by omission of "first edition" from verso of title page. Reprinted: New York: Harcourt, Brace and Co., 1954. History of printings as a single volume, with quantities printed, is as follows:
   (1) First edition, September 1947, 750
   (2) First reprinting, August 1954, 1000
   (3) Second reprinting, May 1961, 500
   (4) Third reprinting, September 1963, 1000.
Reprinted in paperback edition: *The Poems of Richard Wilbur* (*see below*).

Ceremony and Other Poems. New York: Harcourt, Brace and Co., 1950. 55 pages. Toronto: George J. McLeod, 1950. Subsequent printings identified by omission of "first edition" from verso of title page. History of printings as a single volume by Harcourt, Brace and Co., with quantities printed, is as follows:
   (1) First edition, October 1950, 1500
   (2) First reprinting, October 1954, 1000

(3) Second reprinting, September 1961, 500
(4) Third reprinting, June 1965, 500.
Reprinted in paperback edition: *The Poems of Richard Wilbur* (*see below*).

Things of This World, Poems by Richard Wilbur. New York: Harcourt, Brace and Co., 1956. 50 pages. Subsequent printings identified by omission of "first edition" from verso of title page. History of printings as a single volume, with quantities printed, is as follows:
(1) First edition, June 1956, 2000
(2) First reprinting, January 1957, 2500
(3) Second reprinting, May 1957, 3000
(4) Third reprinting, May 1964, 1100
(5) Fourth reprinting, July 1968, 1000.
Reprinted in paperback edition: *The Poems of Richard Wilbur* (*see below*).

Poems 1943–1956. London: Faber and Faber, 1957. 136 pages. Second impression, 1964, identified as such on verso of title page. Contains selections from *The Beautiful Changes, Ceremony*, and *Things of This World*, three of which have undergone minor revisions, plus a passage from Wilbur's translation of Molière's *Misanthrope* and a lyric from *Candide* (*see below*, 2).

Advice to a Prophet and other poems. New York: Harcourt, Brace & World, Inc., 1961. 64 pages. London: Faber and Faber, 1962. 64 pages. Subsequent printings identified by omission of "first edition" from verso of title page. History of printings as a single volume by Harcourt, Brace & World, Inc., with quantities printed, is as follows:
(1) First edition, October 1961, 2000
(2) First reprinting, January 1962, 2000
(3) Second reprinting, February 1967, 1000.

Reprinted in paperback edition: *The Poems of Richard Wilbur* (*see below*).

The Poems of Richard Wilbur. New York: Harcourt, Brace & World, Inc., 1963. 227 pages, A paperback edition, in which are collected all of the poems of *The Beautiful Changes, Ceremony, Things of This World*, and *Advice to a Prophet*, exactly as originally printed. Subsequent printings identified by omission of "'first edition" from verso of title page. History of printings, with quantities printed, is as follows:

(1) First edition, July 1963, 6000
(2) First reprinting, May 1965, 2000
(3) Second reprinting, February 1966, 2000
(4) Third reprinting, October 1966, 2000
(5) Fourth reprinting, February 1967, 6100
(6) Fifth reprinting, August 1969, 4000.

Complaint. New York: Phoenix Book Shop, 1968. 12 pages. An edition of 26 copies lettered *A* to *Z*, not for sale, and 100 copies numbered and signed by the author. The Library of Congress copy was neither signed, numbered, nor lettered. The single poem that constitutes this volume appeared originally in the *New Yorker* (*see below*, B, 2, No. 195), and was reprinted in *Walking to Sleep* (*see below*).

Walking to Sleep, New Poems and Translations. New York: Harcourt, Brace & World, Inc., 1969. 79 pages. This first edition was printed in February 1969, in a quantity of 3000.

Digging for China; *a poem*. Illustrated by William Pène Du Bois. Garden City, N. Y.: Doubleday, 1970. 32 pages. First edition. Colored illustrations.

2. Volumes of translation, musical lyrics, and compilation
Listed chronologically.

A Bestiary. Compiled by Richard Wilbur. Illustrations by
   Alexander Calder. New Work: Printed at the Spiral Press
   for Pantheon Books, 1955. 80 pages, 60 drawings, boxed.
   A limited edition of 800 numbered copies, signed by the
   compiler and the artist. "An anthology of prose and poetry
   on various beasts, with drawings for each animal."
   Toronto: McClelland & Stewart, 1955. Limited edition.

The Misanthrope, Molière. A verse translation by Richard
   Wilbur, with six line drawings by Enrico Arno. New York:
   Harcourt, Brace and Co., 1955. 152 pages. A limited
   edition, numbered and signed by Richard Wilbur. London:
   Faber and Faber, 1958. 140 pages. Reprinted in paperback
   edition: *The Misanthrope and Tartuffe*, 1965 (*see below*).
   Reprinted in a single volume: London: Methuen, 1967.
   84 pages. Part of Methuen's Theatre Classics series, with
   an Introductory Note by Martin Turnell.

Candide, A Comic Operetta Based on Voltaire's Satire. Lyrics
   by Richard Wilbur, Book by Lillian Hellman, Score by
   Leonard Bernstein, Other Lyrics by John Latouche and
   Dorothy Parker. First presented December 1, 1956, at the
   Martin Beck Theater, New York City. New York: Random
   House, 1957. 143 pages, photos. Toronto: Random
   House, 1957. Vocal score published: New York: G.
   Schirmer, Inc., 1958. Operetta reprinted in paperback
   edition: New York: Bard Books / Avon Books, 1970. 156
   pages. Includes Wilbur's "Pangloss's Song," which had
   been removed after the try-out in Boston and was not
   published in the Random House edition (although printed

in *Advice to a Prophet* [*see above*, 1]), plus some other material in Act I, scene ii not by Wilbur that had also been removed. First printing, February 1970. Condensations of the operetta, including some of the lyrics, were published in *The Best Plays of 1956–1957*, ed. Louis Kronenberger. New York: Dodd, Mead & Co., 1957, pp. 148–169; and *Broadway's Best, 1957*, ed. John A. Chapman. Garden City, N. Y.: Doubleday & Co., Inc., 1957. A record of the operetta is also available (*see below*, G).

The Pelican from a Bestiary of 1120. Translated by Richard Wilbur . . . from Philippe de Thaun's Anglo-Norman bestiary of 1120. Initials by Margaret Adams. Stanbrook Abbey, Worcestershire. Privately printed for Philip Hofer at the Stanbrook Abbey Press, 1963. 5 pages. The single poem that constitutes this volume appeared originally in the *Hudson Review* (*see below*, B, 2, No. 122), in *A Bestiary* in 1955 (*see above*), and in *Things of This World* in 1956 (*see above*, 1).

Tartuffe, Molière. A verse translation by Richard Wilbur. New York: Harcourt, Brace & World, Inc., 1963. 106 pages. London: Faber and Faber, 1964. 106 pages. Don Mills, Ontario: Longmans Canada, 1964. History of printings by Harcourt, Brace & World, Inc., with quantities printed, is as follows:

(1) First edition, July 1963, 3000
(2) First reprinting, May 1966, 1000.

Reprinted in two paperback editions: *The Misanthrope and Tartuffe*, 1965 (*see below*); and as a single volume: New York: Harcourt, Brace & World, Inc., 1968. 164 pages. This first edition was printed in November 1967, in a quantity of 50,000.

6

The Misanthrope and Tartuffe, Molière. Translated into English
verse by Richard Wilbur. Drawings by Enrico Arno.
New York: Harcourt, Brace & World, Inc., 1965. 326
pages. A paperback edition of the two translations described
above. Subsequent printings identified by omission of "first
edition" from verso of title page. History of printings,
with quantities printed, is as follows:
  (1) First edition, September 1965, 8000
  (2) First reprinting, February 1966, 8000
  (3) Second reprinting, May 1966, 4000
  (4) Third reprinting, March 1967, 10,000
  (5) Fourth reprinting, September 1967, 5000
  (6) Fifth reprinting, February 1968, 8000
  (7) Sixth reprinting, August 1968, 7000
  (8) Seventh reprinting, January 1969, 6000
  (9) Eighth reprinting, August 1969, 6000.

3. Books edited

Listed chronologically.

Modern American & Modern British Poetry. Ed. Louis
Untermeyer, in consultation with Karl Shapiro and Richard
Wilbur. New York: Harcourt, Brace and Co., 1955. 697
pages. Further revised in 1959.

Poe, Complete poems, with an introduction and notes by the
General Editor [Richard Wilbur]. Laurel Poetry Series,
New York: Dell Publishing Co., Inc., 1959. 159 pages.

Poems, William Shakespeare. Eds. Richard Wilbur & Alfred
Harbage. Baltimore: Penguin Books, 1966. 184 pages.
Introduction and notes.

4. Other

Loudmouse. Illustrated by Don Almquist. New York: Crowell-
    Collier Press, 1963. Unpaged. London: Collier-Macmillan,
    1963. Reissued in new format with new illustrations,
    1968. Unpaged.

B. Individual poems (including translations)

1. Contents of volumes of poetry

Listed in order of appearance. Quotation marks have been used around titles of poems *only* if used by Wilbur as part of the title. Since all of the poems in Wilbur's first four volumes (*The Beautiful Changes*, *Ceremony*, *Things of This World*, and *Advice to a Prophet*) were reprinted in *The Poems of Richard Wilbur* without change (*see above*, A, 1), there seems no point in including this volume here or in part 2, below.

The Beautiful Changes
Cigales
Water Walker
Tywater
Mined Country
Potato
First Snow in Alsace
On the Eyes of an SS Officer
Place Pigalle
Violet and Jasper
The Peace of Cities
The Giaour and the Pacha
Up, Jack
In a Bird Sanctuary
June Light
A Song
The Walgh-Vogel

14

2. Publication history

Listed chronologically. The following abbreviations are used to indicate successive printings:

The Beautiful Changes	BC	*Poems 1943–1956*	*P43–56*
Ceremony	CY	*Advice to a Prophet*	*AP*
A Bestiary	BY	*Tartuffe*	*T*
The Misanthrope	M	*Walking to Sleep*	*WS*
Things to This World	*TTW*		

Revision of a preceding version is indicated by (r); if there is no mark the version is the same as the immediately preceding one. I define revision as a change of thought or expression, including change of title; corrections of errors, variants in spelling (including capitalization), and punctuation have been disregarded.

Each poem is numbered. Quotation marks have been used around titles of poems at the beginning of each citation *only* if used by Wilbur as part of the title.

1. The Hoover and the Hamilton. . . . *Touchstone* [Amherst College student magazine], IV (December 1938), 8.

2. The nicest man I've ever seen. . . . *Touchstone*, IV (December 1938), 9.

3. A noble fellow, we are told. . . . *Touchstone*, IV (December 1938), 9.

4. Heywood. *Touchstone*, IV (April 1939), 12.

5. Dorothy. *Touchstone*, IV (April 1939), 12.

6. Mark. *Touchstone*, IV (April 1939), 13.

7. Westbrook. *Touchstone*, IV (April 1939), 13.

8. Italy: Maine. *Saturday Evening Post*, CCXVII (September 23, 1944), 37.

9. Water Walker. (a) *Foreground*, I (Spring–Summer 1946), 99–102. (b) *BC*. (c) *P43–56*.

10. Place Pigalle. (a) *Foreground*, I (Spring–Summer 1946), 102. (b) *BC*.

11. The Regatta. (a) *Foreground*, I (Spring–Summer 1946), 103–104. (b) *BC*.

12. Potato. (a) *Foreground*, I (Spring–Summer 1946), 104–105. (b) *BC*. (c) *P43–56*.

13. Mined Country, (a) *Foreground*, I (Spring–Summer 1946), 105–106. (b) *BC*. (c) *P43–56*.

14. In a Bird Sanctuary. (a) *Foreground*, I (Spring–Summer 1946), 106–107. (b) *BC* (r). (c) *P43–56*.

15. Cigales. (a) *Accent*, VI (Summer 1946), 241–242. (b) *BC*. (c) *P43–56* (r).

16. Grace. (a) *Accent*, VI (Summer 1946), 242–243. (b) *BC*. (c) *P43–56* (r) .

17. A Song. (a) *Accent*, VI (Summer 1946), 243–244. (b) *BC*.

18. The Beautiful Changes. (a) *Harvard Advocate*, CXXX (April 1947), 7. (b) *Junior Bazaar*, III (November 1947), 106. (c) *BC*. (d) *P43–56*.

19. The Walgh-Vogel. (a) *Harvard Advocate*, CXXX (April 1947), 7. (b) *New Directions 10 in Prose and Poetry*, ed. James Laughlin (New York: New Directions, 1948), p. 463. (c) *BC*. [Although this and the other poems that appeared in *New Directions 10* were actually published in *BC* (1947) before they were in *New Directions 10*, they had apparently been submitted to and accepted by the latter before arrangements for *BC* were made. The publication of *New Directions 10* appears to have been delayed, and was probably originally scheduled for 1947: *New Directions 9* was published in 1946. In any event, *New*

Directions 10 is acknowledged as a place of prior publication in *BC.*]

20. Objects. (a) *Harvard Advocate*, CXXX (April 1947), 8. (b) *BC.* (c) *P43–56.*

21. Tywater. (a) *Harvard Advocate*, CXXX (April 28, 1947), 9. (b) *BC.* (c) *P43–56.*

22. & [Ampersand]. *BC.*

23. Attention Makes Infinity. *BC.*

24. Bell Speech. (a) *BC.* (b) *P43–56.*

25. Caserta Garden. *BC.*

26. A Dubious Night. *BC.*

27. For Ellen. *BC.*

28. The Giaour and the Pacha. (a) *BC.* (b) *P43–56.*

29. June Light. (a) *BC.* (b) *P43–56.*

30. Lightness. (a) *BC.* (b) *P43–56.*

31. The Melongene. *BC.*

32. My Father Paints the Summer. (a) *BC.* (b) *P43–56.*

33. O. *BC.*

34. On the Eyes of an SS Officer. *BC.*

35. The Peace of Cities. (a) *BC.* (b) *P43–56.*

36. Poplar, Sycamore. (a) *BC.* (b) *P43–56.*

37. Praise in Summer. (a) *BC.* (b) *P43–56.*

38. Sun and Air. *BC.*

39. Sunlight Is Imagination. *BC.*

40. Superiorities. *BC*.

41. Two Songs in a Stanza of Beddoes'. *BC*.

42. Up, Jack. *BC*.

43. Violet and Jasper. *BC*.

44. The Waters. *BC*.

45. Winter Spring. *BC*.

46. Folk Tune. (a) *New Directions 10*, p. 460 [*see above*, no. 19]. (b) *BC*.

47. A Simplification. (a) *New Directions 10*, p. 461 [*see above*, no. 19]. (b) *BC*.

48. First Snow in Alsace. (a) *New Directions 10*, p. 461 [*see above*, no. 19]. (b) *BC*. (c) *P43–56*.

49. A Dutch Courtyard. (a) *New Directions 10*, p. 462 [*see above*, no. 19]. (b) *BC*. (c) *P43–56*.

50. L'Etoile. (a) *New Directions 10*, p. 463 [*see above*, no. 19]. (b) *BC*. (c) *P43–56*.

51. Henri Pichette: Apoem I. (a) *Transition Forty-Eight*, No. 4 (1948), pp. 60–65 [French-English]. (b) *Little Treasury of World Poetry*, ed. Hubert Creekmore (New York: Charles Scribners' Sons, 1952), pp. 671–673 (r).

52. Ceremony. (a) *Poetry*, LXXI (February 1948), 231–232. (b) *CY* (r). (c) *P43–56*.

53. A Simile for Her Smile. (a) *Poetry*, LXXI (February 1948), 232. (b) *CY*. (c) *P43–56*.

54. The Death of a Toad. (a) *Poetry*, LXXI (February 1948), 233. (b) *CY*. (c) *BY*. (d) *P43–56*.

55. Five Women Bathing in Moonlight. (a) *Poetry*, LXXI (February 1948), 234. (b) *CY* (r).

56. Wellfleet: The House. (a) *Poetry*, LXXI (February 1948), 235. (b) *CY*.

57. Conjuration. (a) *Poetry*, LXXI (February 1948), 236. (b) *CY*. (c) *P43–56*.

58. Museum Piece. (a) *Poetry*, LXXI (February 1948), 237. (b) *CY*. (c) *P43–56*.

59. First Forth Gewat [Part I of Notes on Heroes (I–IV)]. *Wake*, VI (Spring 1948), 80. [A translation of lines 210–224 of *Beowulf*.]

60. Beowulf [Part II of Notes on Heroes (I–IV)]. (a) *Wake*, VI (Spring 1948), 80–81. (b) *CY*. (c) *P43–56*.

61. "It Is Time To Reveal Joy" [Part III of Notes on Heroes (I–IV)]. *Wake*, VI (Spring 1948), 82.

62. Still, Citizen Sparrow [Part IV of Notes on Heroes (I–IV)]. (a) *Wake*, VI (Spring 1948), 83. (b) *CY*. (c) *P43–56*.

63. Pity. (a) *Partisan Review*, XV (May 1948), 549. (b) *CY*. (c) *P43–56*.

64. Grasse: The Olive Trees. (a) *New Yorker*, XXIV (June 26, 1948), 28. (b) *CY*. (c) *P43–56*.

65. Lament. (a) *Wake*, VII (1948), 86. (b) *CY*. (c) *P43–56*.

66. Then. (a) *Botteghe Oscure*, II (1948), 303. (b) *Quarterly Review of Literature*, V (Fall 1950), 223. (c) *CY* (r). (d) *P43–56*.

67. From the Lookout Rock. (a) *Botteghe Oscure*, II (1948), 303–305. (b) *Imagi*, V (1949), 6–7. (c) *CY*.

68. The Avowal, *from the French of Villiers de l'Isle Adam.*
    (a) *Yale French Studies,* I (Fall–Winter 1948), 118.
    (b) *CY.*

69. The Gifts, *from the French of Villiers de l'Isle Adam.* (a)
    Yale French Studies, I (Fall–Winter 1948), 118. (b) *CY.*

70. Driftwood. (a) *Poetry,* LXXIII (December 1948),
    125–126. (b) *CY.* (c) *P43–56.*

71. We. *Poetry,* LXXIII (December 1948), 127–128.

72. To an American Poet Just Dead. (a) *Poetry,* LXXIII
    (December 1948), 128–129. (b) *CY.*

73. Weather Bird. *Poetry,* LXXIII (December 1948), 129–130.

74. Tears for the Rich. *American Letters,* I (December 1948),
    12.

75. Natural Song. (a) *American Scholar,* XVIII (Winter
    1948–49), 76–77. (b) *Kavita,* XVI (December 1950),
    7–8 (r).

76. Edgar Degas: Sonnet. *Transition Forty-Nine,* No. 5 (1949),
    pp. 86–87 [French-English].

77. Year's End. (a) *New Yorker,* XXIV (January 1, 1949), 26.
    (b) *CY* (r). (c) *P43–56.*

78. Games One. (a) *American Letters,* I (February 1949), 13
    [titled "The Asterisk"]. (b) *CY* (r).

79. The Puritans. (a) *Harvard Advocate,* CXXXII (February
    28, 1949), 7. (b) *CY* (r). (c) *P43–56.*

80. Giacometti. (a) *Tiger's Eye,* No. 7 (March 1949),
    pp. 61–62. (b) *CY.* (c) *P43–56.*

81. Juggler. (a) *New Yorker*, XXV (April 16, 1949), 28. (b) *CY*. (c) *Mandrake*, II (Autumn & Winter 1954-55), 316 (r). (d) *P43–56* (r).

82. ? [Question Mark]. *American Letters*, I (May 1949), 1.

83. The Terrace, (a) *Inventario* (Florence), II (Summer 1949), 50-53 [Italian-English]. (b) *CY* (r). (c) *P43–56.*

84. La Rose des Vents. (a) *Hopkins Review*, III (Fall 1949), 18. (b) *CY*. (c) *P43–56.*

85. Western Express. *Glass Hill*, October 1949 [there are no volume or page numbers for this magazine].

86. Marché aux Oiseaux. (a) *Virginia Quarterly Review*, XXV (Winter 1949), 60. (b) *Kavita*, XVI (December 1950), 6–7. (c) *CY*. (d) *P43–56.*

87. Nightfalls. *Voices*, No. 136 (Winter 1949), p. 9.

88. Francis Ponge: The Fire. *Transition Fifty*, No. 6 (1950), pp. 75–76.

89. Francis Ponge: The Notebook of the Pine-Woods (*Extracts*). *Transition Fifty*, No. 6 (1950), pp. 76–77.

90. Francis Ponge: The Rain. *Transition Fifty*, No. 6 (1950), pp. 77–78.

91. Francis Ponge: Fauna and Flora. *Transition Fifty*, No. 6 (1950), pp. 80–86.

92. Parable. (a) *Botteghe Oscure*, V (1950), 408. (b) *CY*. (c) *P43–56.*

93. A Problem from Milton. (a) *Botteghe Oscure*, V (1950), 408–409. (b) *CY*. (c) *P43–56.*

94. Clearness. (a) *New Yorker*, XXVI (August 12, 1950), 24. (b) *CY* (r). (c) *P43–56.*

95. Castless and Distances. (a) *Poetry*, LXXVI (September 1950), 311–315. (b) *CY*. (c) *P43–56*.

96. A Courtyard Thaw. (a) *Poetry*, LXXVI (September 1950), 315–316. (b) *CY*. (c) *P43–56*.

97. "A World Without Objects Is a Sensible Emptiness." (a) *Poetry*, LXXVI (September 1950), 316–317. (b) *CY*. (c) *P43–56*.

98. Part of a Letter. (a) *Poetry*, LXXVI (September 1950), 317–318. (b) *CY*. (c) *P43–56*.

99. The Sirens. (a) *New Yorker*, XXVI (September 9, 1950), 36. (b) *CY*.

100. A Glance from the Bridge. (a) *Poetry New York*, No. 3 (Fall 1950), p. 36. (b) *CY*. (c) *P43–56*.

101. The Pardon. (a) *Poetry New York*, No. 3 (Fall 1950), pp. 36–37. (b) *CY*. (c) *P43–56*.

102. Flumen Tenebrarum. (a) *Quarterly Review of Literature*, V (Fall 1950), 223. (b) *CY*. (c) *P43–56*.

103. The Good Servant. (a) *Quarterly of Literature*, V (Fall 1950), 223. (b) *CY*. (c) *P43–56*.

104. Epistemology. (a) *CY*. (b) *P43–56*.

105. Games Two. *CY*.

106. He Was. (a) *CY*. (b) *P43–56*.

107. Ode to Pleasure, *from the French of La Fontaine*. (a) *CY*. (b) *P43–56*.

108. In the Elegy Season. (a) *New Yorker*, XXVI (November 4, 1950), 48. (b) *CY*. (c) *P43–56*.

109. Speech for the Repeal of the McCarran Act. (a) *Origin*, III (Fall 1951), 133. (b) *TTW* (r).

110. Beasts. (a) *Botteghe Oscure*, IX (1952), 249. (b) *Hudson Review*, VI (Spring 1953), 48. (c) *Mandrake*, II Autumn & Winter 1954–55), 317–318. (d) *BY*. (e) *TTW*. (f) *P43–56*.

111. Boy at the Window. (a) *New Yorker*, XXVII (January 5, 1952), 28. (b) *TTW*. (c) *P43–56*.

112. Digging for China. (a) *Beloit Poetry Journal*, II (Spring 1952), 23–24. (b) *TTW*. (c) *P43–56* (r). (d) *Digging for China; a poem* [*see above*, A, 1] (r).

113. Apology .(a) *Beloit Poetry Journal*, II (Spring 1952), 24. (b) *TTW* (r). (c) *P43–56*.

114. The Beacon. (a) *New Yorker*, XXVIII (May 17, 1952), 36. (b) *TTW*. (c) *P43–56*.

115. Exeunt. (a) *New Yorker*, XXVIII (September 20, 1952), 36 [titled "Exodus"]. (b) *TTW* (r). (c) *P43–56*.

116. A Chronic Condition. (a) *Poetry*, LXXXI (October 1952), 87. (b) *TTW* (r). (c) *P43–56*.

117. The Nature of the Siren. *New Mexico Quarterly*, XXII (Winter 1952), 421.

118. Looking Into History. (a) *Botteghe Oscure*, XII (1953), 215–217. (b) *Audience*, II (1955), 6–7. (c) *TTW*. (d) *P43–56*.

119. Statues. (a) *Contemporary Poetry*, XIII (1953), 17. (b) *Paris Review*, I (Summer 1953), 56–57. (c) *TTW*. (d) *P43–56*.

120. Merlin Enthralled. (a) *New Yorker*, XXIX (March 21, 1953), 38. (b) *TTW* (r). (c) *P43–56*.

121. After the Last Bulletins. (a) *New Yorker*, XXIX (April 4, 1953), 32. (b) *New Poems by American Poets*, ed. Rolfe Humphries (New York: Ballantine Books, 1953), p. 162 (r).

122. Philippe de Thaun: The Pelican. (a) *Hudson Review*, VI (Spring 1953), 49–50. (b) *BY*. (c) *TTW*. (d) *P43–56*. (e) *The Pelican from a Bestiary of 1120* [*see above*, A, 2]. (r).

123. The Nature of the Whale. (a) *Hudson Review*, VI (Spring 1953), 50–51. (b) *BY* (r).

124. Francis Jammes: A Prayer to Go to Paradise with the Donkeys. (a) *Furioso*, VIII (Spring 1953), 40–41. (b) *BY*. (c) *TTW*. (d) *P43–56*.

125. A Voice from Under the Table. (a) *Inventario* (Florence), V (January–September 1953), 62-63. (b) *Kenyon Review*, XVI (Winter 1954), 79–80 (r). (c) *TTW*. (d) *P43–56*.

126. Paul Valéry: Helen. (a) *Wake*, XII (1953), 83. (b) *TTW* (r). (c) *P43–56*.

127. A Black November Turkey. (a) *New Yorker*, XXIX (November 21, 1953), 42. (b) *TTW* (r). (c) *P43–56*.

128. *The Misanthrope* (Act I—Scene II). (a) *New World Writing, Fifth Mentor Selection* (New York: New American Library, 1954), pp. 88–93. (b) *M* (r).

129. Marginalia. (a) *Poetry*, LXXXIII (February 1954), 265. (b) *Mandrake*, (Autumn & Winter 1954–55), 319. (c) *TTW*. (d) *P43–56*.

130. Lamarck Elaborated. (a) *Poetry*, LXXXIII (February 1954), 266. (b) *Mandrake*, II (Autumn & Winter 1954–55), 318. (c) *TTW*. (d) *P43–56*.

131. A Plain Song for Comadre. (a) *Poetry*, LXXXIII
(February 1954), 267–268. (b) *TTW*. (c) *P43–56*.

132. Mind. (a) *Trinity Review*, VIII (May 1954), 46. (b)
Mandrake, II (Autumn & Winter 1954–55), 317. (c)
TTW. (d) *P43–56*.

133. Charles Baudelaire: L'Invitation au Voyage. (a) *Imagi*,
VI (1954), 3. (b) *The Flowers of Evil*, eds. Marthiel &
Joseph Mathews (New York: New Directions ,1955),
pp. 67–69 [as was the case in no. 19, above, this may be the
place of original publication, rather than *Imagi*]. (c)
TTW. (d) *P43–56*.

134. Charles Baudelaire: The Albatross. (a) *Flowers*, p. 10
[*see above*, no. 133]. (b) *Fifty Great Poets*, ed Milton
Crane (New York: Bantam Books, 1961), p. 409.

135. Charles Baudelaire: Correspondences. (a) *Flowers*, p. 12
[*see above*, no. 133]. (b) *Fifty Great Poets*, p. 409 [*see
above*, no. 134].

136. Jean de la Fontaine: The Grasshopper and the Ant. (a)
BY. (b) *Poems from France*, ed. William Jay Smith
(New York: Thomas Y. Crowell Co., 1967), pp. 49–50.

137. *The Misanthrope*, Act III, Scene v. (a) *M*. (b) *P43–56*.

138. All These Birds. (a) *New Yorker*, XXXI (May 7, 1955),
44. (b) *TTW*. (c) *P43–56*.

139. John Chrysostom. (a) *Nimbus*, III, Double Issue (Summer
1955), 84. (b) *TTW*. (c) *P43–56*.

140. The Mill. (a) *Nimbus*, III, Double Issue (Summer 1955),
84–85. (b) *TTW*. (c) *P43–56*.

141. Love Calls Us to the Things of This World. (a) *Botteghe Oscure*, XVI (Autumn 1955), 244–245. (b) *Audience*, IV, Double Issue (May 4, 1956), 4. (c) *TTW*. (d) *P43–56*.

142. For the New Railway Station in Rome. (a) *Botteghe Oscure*, XVI (Autumn 1955), 245–246. (b) *TTW*. (c) *P43–56*.

143. Sonnet. (a) *Botteghe Oscure*, XVI (Autumn 1955), 246–247. (b) *TTW*. (c) *P43–56*.

144. Piazza di Spanga, Early Morning. (a) *Botteghe Oscure*, XVI (Autumn 1955), 247. (b) *TTW* (r). (c) *Commentary*, XXIII (May 1957), 457. (d) *P43–56*.

145. A Baroque Wall-Fountain in the Villa Sciarra. (a) *New Yorker*, XXXI (October 8, 1955), 42. (b) *TTW* (r). (c) *P43–56*.

146. Fall in Corrales. (a) *Nation*, CLXXXII (January 21, 1956), 53. (b) *AP* (r).

147. René Char: Les Transparents. (a) *Poetry*, LXXXVII (March 1956), 316–322. (b) *Hypnos Waking*, trans. Jackson Mathews and others (New York: Random House, 1956), pp. 9–19.

148. An Event. (a) *TTW*. (b) *P43–56*.

149. Altitudes. (a) *Partisan Review*, XXIII (Winter 1956), 45–46. (b) *TTW*. (c) *P43–56*.

150. Loves of the Puppets. (a) *New Yorker*, XXXIII (April 13, 1957), 40. (b) *AP*.

151. Pangloss's Song: A Comic-Opera Lyric. (a) *Partisan Review*, XXIV (Spring 1957), 210–211. (b) *New Poems*

by American Poets #2, ed. Rolfe Humphries (New York: Ballantine Books, 1957), pp. 167–168 (r). (c) *P43–56* (r). (d) *AP*. (e) *Candide*, 1970 edition, pp. 47–48 [*see above*, A, 2].

152. Two Voices in a Meadow. (a) *New Poems* #2, p. 168 [*see above*, no. 151]. (b) *New Yorker*, XXXIII (August 17, 1957), 26. (c) *AP*.

153. Someone Talking to Himself. (a) *New Yorker*, XXXIV (June 14, 1958), 34. (b) *AP*.

154. A Fire-Truck. (a) *New Yorker*, XXXIV (October 25, 1958), 44. (b) *AP*.

155. She. (a) *Atlantic*, CCII (November 1958), 42. (b) *Evergreen Review*, No. 17 (March–April 1961), pp 61–62. (c) *AP*.

156. Advice to a Prophet. (a) *New Yorker*, XXXV (April 4, 1959), 40. (b) *AP*.

157. Another Voice. (a) *Transatlantic Review*, No. 1 (Summer 1959), pp. 7–8. (b) *AP* (r).

158. Jorge Guillén: The Horses. (a) *American Scholar*, XXVIII (Summer 1959), 296. (b) *AP*.

159. A Grasshopper. (a) *New Yorker*, XXXV (August 22, 1959), 34. (b) *AP* (r).

160. Two Quatrains for First Frost. (a) *New Yorker*, XXXV (October 31, 1959), 41. (b) *AP* (r).

161. Gérard de Nerval: Antéros. (a) *Quagga*, I (1960), 15. (b) *AP*.

162. In the Smoking-Car. (a) *New Yorker*, XXXV (January 2, 1960), 32. (b) *AP*.

163. A Summer Morning. (a) *Poets at Wesleyan*, based on a
Reading at Wesleyan University, 1959. Sponsored by
Transatlantic Review, printed by The Bond Press,
Hartford Conn., p. 68. [The volume includes selections by
Willis Barnstone, Richard Wilbur and several others.]
(b) *New Yorker*, XXXVI (August 6, 1960), 32 (r). (c)
AP.

164. October Maples, Portland. (a) *New Yorker*, XXXVI
(October 22, 1960), 46. (b) *AP* (r).

165. Jorge Guillén: Death, from a Distance. (a) *Atlantic*,
CCVII (January 1961), 129 [in "Jorge Guillén, A Poet of
This Time," by Archibald Macleish]. (b) *AP*.

166. Stop. (a) *New Yorker*, XXXVI (January 21, 1961), 44.
(b) *AP*.

167. Ballade for the Duke of Orléans. (a) *New Yorker*,
XXXVII (April 1, 1961), 36. (b) *AP*.

168. Shame. (a) *Between Worlds*, I (Spring–Summer 1961),
214. (b) *AP*. (c) *Richard Wilbur Reading His Poetry*,
Caedmon TC 1248 [*see below*, G] (r).

169. Next Door. (a) *New Yorker*, XXXVII (May 6, 1961),
40. (b) *AP*.

170. The Undead. (a) *New Yorker*, XXXVII (June 3, 1961),
30. (b) *AP*.

171. A Hole in the Floor. (a) *New Yorker*, XXXVII (July 1,
1961), 32. (b) *AP*.

172. Gemini. (a) *Poetry*, XCVIII (August 1961), 275. (b) *AP*.

173. To Ishtar. (a) *Poetry*, XCVIII (August 1961), 276. (b)
AP.

174. Anna Akhmatova: Lot's Life. (a) *Paris Review*, VII (Summer / Fall 1961), 125. (b) *WS*.

175. Anna Akhmatova: To N. V. Rikov-Gukovski. *Paris Review*, VII (Summer / Fall 1961), 126.

176. Molière: *Tartuffe*, Act I, Scenes iii–v. (a) *Poetry*, XCVIII (September 1961), 369–375. (b) *AP* [scene iv only]. (c) *T* (r).

177. The Aspen and the Stream. (a) *New Yorker*, XXXVII (September 2, 1961), 26. (b) *AP*.

178. Junk. (a) *Nation*, CXCIII (September 2, 1961), 126. (b) *AP* (r).

179. Salvatore Quasimodo: The Agrigentum Road. *AP*.

180. A Christmas Hymn. *AP*.

181. Molière: *Tartuffe*, Act III, Scenes i–iii. (a) *Poetry*, CI (October–November 1962), 133–140. (b) *T* (r).

182. Eight Riddles from Symphosius. (a) *Choice*, No. 2 (1962), p. 18. (b) *AP*. [Again, as in no. 19, above, there is some confusion about the order of publication, but *Choice* is listed as a place of prior publication in *AP*.]

183. A Poem of Dedication for Lincoln Center. *Lincoln Center Souvenir Booklet*, September 23, 1962; reprinted in *New York Times*, CXII (September 24, 1962), 34.

184. Molière: *Tartuffe*, Act II. (a) *Drama Critique*, V (Fall 1962), 132–141. (b) *T* (r).

185. Leaving. *Poetry in Crystal, by Steuben Glass*. Interpretations in crystal of thirty-one new poems by contemporary American poets. New York: Spiral Press, 1963, p. 70. [In a letter to me dated February 22, 1970, Wilbur

suggested that the word "pediments" in line 11 be replaced by "pedestals."]

186. Andrei Voznesensky: Foggy Street. (a) *Encounter*, XX (April 1963), 57 [in "Eight Poems," trans. W. H. Auden, Stanley Kunitz, and Richard Wilbur, 52–58; in "New Voices in Russian Writing, an Anthology," eds Patricia Blake and Max Hayward, 27–90]. (b) Voznesensky, *Antiworlds*, eds. Patricia Blake and Max Hayward (New York: Basic Books, Inc., 1966), p. 35 (r) .(c) Voznesensky, *Antiworlds and "The Fifth Ace,"* eds. Patricia Blake and Max Hayward (Garden City, N. Y.: Anchor Books, 1967), p. 81. (d) *WS*.

187. Andrei Voznesensky: Antiworlds. (a) *Encounter*, XX (April 1963), 58 [*see above*, no. 186]. (b) *Antiworlds*, 1966, p. 40 [*see above*, no. 186] (r). (c) *The Penguin Book of Modern Verse Translation*, ed. George Steiner (Baltimore: Penguin Books, 1966), p. 268 (r). (d) *Antiworlds*, 1967, p. 93 [*see above*, no. 186] (r). (a) *WS*.

188. Molière: *Tartuffe*, Act IV. (a) *Massachusetts Review*, IV (Spring 1963), 582–596. (b) *T* (r).

189. The Lilacs. (a) *New York Review of Books*, I (December 12, 1963), 2. (b) *WS*.

190. A Riddle. (a) *Festschrift for Marianne Moore's Seventy-Seventh Birthday*, ed. Tambimuttu (New York: Tambimuttu & Mass, 1964), p. 116. (b) *WS* (r).

191. The Proof. (a) *Atlantic*, CCXIII (March 1964), 62. (b) *WS*.

192. Seed Leaves. (a) *New Yorker*, XL (April 4, 1964), 42. (b) *WS* (r).

193. Charles D'Orléans: Rondeau. (a) *Penny Poems from Midwestern University* (Wichita Falls, Texas), I (October 30, 1964) [no pagination; the whole issue is one page]. (b) *WS*.

194. François Villon: Ballade of the Ladies of Time Past. (a) *Poetry*, CV (November 1964), 81–82. (b) *WS* (r).

195. Complaint. (a) *New Yorker*, XL (January 23, 1965), 36. (b) *Complaint* [*see above*, A, 1] (r). (c) *WS*.

196. On the Marginal Way. (a) *New Yorker*, XLI (September 25, 1965), 48. (b) *WS*.

197. Rillons, Rillettes. *New Yorker*, XLI (January 29, 1966), 28.

198. Andrei Voznesensky: Dead Still. (a) *New York Review of Books*, VI (April 14, 1966), 4. (b) *Antiworlds*, 1966, p. 22 [*see above*, no. 186]. (c) *Antiworlds*, 1967, p. 55 [*see above*, no. 186]. (d) *WS*.

199. Under Cygnus. (a) *Nation*, CCIII (December 19, 1966), 675. (b) *WS*.

200. Joachim Du Bellay: Heureux, Qui, Comme, Ulysse. *Vassar Review*, Winter 1966, p. 24. [The title of the poem was printed as shown above; however, in a letter to me dated February 22, 1970, Wilbur pointed out that the comma between "Comme" and "Ulysse" should not be there.]

201. A Miltonic Sonnet for Mr. Johnson. (a) *New York Review of Books*, VIII (April 6, 1967), 28. (b) *WS* (r).

202. A Wood. (a) *New Yorker*, XLIII (May 6, 1967), 42. (b) *WS*.

203. Fern-Beds in Hampshire County. (a) *Poetry Northwest*, VIII (Summer 1967), 21. (b) *WS*.

204. Walking to Sleep. (a) *New Yorker*, XLIII (December 23, 1967), 32–33. (b) *WS* (r).

205. Jorge Luís Borges: Ewigkeit. (a) *Artes Hispanicus / Hispanic Arts*, I (Winter / Spring 1968). [I have been unable to corroborate this citation, and believe the poem may have been intended for publication but never published because of the magazine's discontinuation.] (b) *WS*.

206. Jorge Luís Borges: Everness. (a) *Artes Hispanicus / Hispanic Arts*, I (Winter /Spring 1968). [*see above*, no. 205.] (b) *WS*.

207. A Postcard for Bob Bly. *Kayak 13*, January 1968, 15.

208. Running. (a) *New Yorker*, XLIV (March 9, 1968), 44. (b) *WS* (r).

209. François Villon: Ballade in Old French. (a) *The Tin Drum* [a Wesleyan University student paper], June 1968. (b) *WS* (r).

210. The Mechanist. (a) *The Tin Drum* [a Wesleyan University student paper], June 1968. (b) *WS* (r).

211. A Late Aubade. (a) *New Yorker*, XLIV (August 3, 1968), 32. (b) *WS*.

212. For K. R. on Her Sixtieth Birthday. (a) *New York Review of Books*, XI (August 22, 1968), 4. (b) *WS*.

213. Playboy. (a) *New York Review of Books*, XI (August 22, 1968), 4. (b) *WS*.

214. In the Field. (a) *New Yorker*, XLIV (September 14, 1968), 60. (b) *WS*.

215. Jorge Luís Borges: Compass. (a) *Atlantic*, CCXXII (October 1968), 80. (b) *WS*.

216. In a Churchyard. (a) *New Yorker*, XLIV (November 23, 1968), 66. (b) *WS*.

217. Thyme Flowering among Rocks. (a) *New Yorker*, XLIV (December 14, 1968), 64. (b) *WS*.

218. François Villon: A Ballade to End With. (a) *Kayak 16* (1968), 12 [titled "Icy se clost le testament"]. (b) *WS* (r).

219. For Dudley. (a) *Hudson Review*, XXI (Winter 1968–69), 644–645. (b) *WS*.

220. Matthew VIII, 28 ff. (a) *Hudson Review*, XXI (Winter 1968–69), 645. (b) *WS*.

221. The Agent. (a) *Quarterly Review of Literature*, XVI (1969), 265–267. (b) *WS*.

222. François Villon: Ballade of Forgiveness. *Hollins Critic*, VI, Special Issue (July 1969), 9.

C. Articles, stories (including translations), and short editorial work

Listed chronologically.

Untitled short story. *Touchstone* [Amherst College student magazine], IV (April 1938), 8.

"War Aces, A Scenario Fraught With Emotion," *Touchstone*, IV (May 1939), 14–15.

"Breaking of the Dream," *Touchstone*, IV (June 1939), 17–18.

"Family Picture," *Touchstone*, V (October 1939), 11, 23, 24, 26.

"Essence Greenling, Man and Poet, –or– Belding Thresher Breaks Through," *Touchstone*, VI (March 1941), 15.

"The Day After the War," *Foreground*, I (Spring–Summer 1948), 108–116.

Villiers de l'Isle Adam: "The Pleasures of Charity," *Quarterly Review of Literature*, IV (1947), 30–35.

Villiers de l'Isle Adam: "The Swan-Killer," *Quarterly Review of Literature*, IV (1947), 36–39.

Explanatory remarks on "Driftwood" and "To an American Poet Just Dead," in *A Critical Supplement to Poetry*, ed. John Frederick Nims, December 1948, pp. 1–9.

"The Genie in the Bottle," in *Mid-Century American Poets*, ed. John Ciardi (New York: Twayne Publishers, 1950), pp. 1–7; reprinted in *Writing Poetry*, ed. John Holmes (Boston: The Writer, Inc., 1960), pp. 120–130.

"The Bottles Become New, Too," *Quarterly Review of Literature*, VII (1953), 186–192.

"A Game of Catch," *New Yorker*, XXIX (July 18, 1953), 74–76; reprinted in *American Accent*, fourteen stories by authors associated with the Bread Loaf Writers' Conference, ed. Elizabeth Abell (New York: Ballantine Books, 1954), pp. 60–64; reprinted in *Prize Stories 1954: The O. Henry Awards*, eds. Paul Engle and Hansford Martin (New York: Doubleday & Co., 1954), pp. 47–50; reprinted in *Stories from the New Yorker 1950–1960* (New York: Simon and Schuster, 1960), pp. 392–395.

Jules Renard: "A Romance," in *French Stories and Tales*, ed. Stanley Geist (New York: Alfred A. Knopf, 1954), pp. 263–272.

"Poetry," selected by Richard Wilbur, *New World Writing, Eighth Mentor Selection* (New York: New American Library, 1955), pp. 148–167.

"Introduction" to *The Misanthrope*, 1955 [*see above*, A, 2]; reprinted in *The Misanthrope and Tartuffe*, 1965, pp. 7–10 [*see above*, A, 2].

"Poetry and the Landscape," in *The New Landscape in Art & Science*, ed. Gyorgy Kepes (Chicago: Paul Theobald & Co., 1956), pp. 86–90.

Commentary on three critiques of "Love Calls Us to the Things of This World," in "A Symposium on Richard Wilbur's 'Love Calls Us to the Things of This World,'" ed. Anthony Ostroff, *Berkeley Review*, I (1957), 47–51; reprinted in *The Contemporary Poet as Artist and Critic: Eight*

Symposia, ed. Anthony Ostroff (Boston: Little, Brown and Co., 1964), pp. 17–21.

"The House of Poe," *Anniversary Lectures 1959,* Reference Department, Library of Congress, Washington, D. C., 1959, pp. 21–38. One of three lectures for 1959 presented under the auspices of the Gertrude Clarke Whittall Poetry and Literature Fund. Reprinted in *The Recognition of Edgar Allan Poe, Selected Criticism Since 1829,* ed. Eric W. Carlson (Ann Arbor: University of Michigan Press, 1966), pp. 254–277; reprinted in *Poe, A Collection of Critical Essays,* ed. Robert Regan (Englewood Cliffs, N. J.: Prentice-Hall, Inc., 1967), pp. 98–120.

"Introduction" to *Poe, Complete poems,* Laurel Poetry Series (New York: Dell Publishing Co., Inc., 1959), pp. 7–39. [*see above,* A, 3].

"Sumptuous Destitution," in *Emily Dickinson: Three Views,* Archibald MacLeish, Louis Bogan, Richard Wilbur. Papers delivered at Amherst College as part of its observance of the Bicentennial celebration of the Town of Amherst, Massachusetts on October 23, 1959 (Amherst: Amherst College Press, 1960), pp. 35–46; reprinted in *Emily Dickinson, A Collection of Critical Essays,* ed. Richard B. Sewall (Englewood Cliffs, N. J.: Prentice-Hall, Inc., 1963), pp. 127–136.

"Edgar Allan Poe, 1809–1849," in *Major Writers of America I,* ed. Perry Miller (New York: Harcourt, Brace & World, Inc., 1962), pp. 369–475. [Introduction, poetry and prose.]

Essay in "The Poet and His Critics: III. A Symposium on Robert Lowell's 'Skunk Hour,' " ed. Anthony Ostroff, in *New World Writing,* No. 21 (Philadelphia and New

York: J. B. Lippincott Co., 1962), pp. 133–137; reprinted in *The Contemporary Poet as Artist and Critic: Eight Symposia*. ed. Anthony Ostroff (Boston: Little, Brown and Co., 1964), pp. 84–87.

"Round About a Poem of Housman's," in *The Moment of Poetry*, ed. Don Cameron Allen (Baltimore: Johns Hopkins University Press, 1962), pp. 73–98. One of the 1961 Percy Graeme Turnbull Memorial Lectures on Poetry, delivered at The Johns Hopkins University. Reprinted in *A Celebration of Poets*, ed. Don Cameron Allen (Baltimore: Johns Hopkins University Press, 1967), pp. 177–202.

Comment on "A Baroque Wall-Fountain in the Villa Sciarra," in *Poet's Choice*, eds. Paul Engle and Joseph Langland (New York: Dial Press, 1962), p. 193.

"Introduction" to *Tartuffe*, 1963, pp. vii–xi [*see above*, A, 2]; reprinted in *The Misanthrope and Tartuffe*, 1965, pp. 159–163 [*see above*, A, 2].

"Edgar Allan Poe," in *The Concise Encyclopedia of English and American Poets and Poetry*, eds. Stephen Spender and Donald Hall (New York: Hawthorn Books, Inc., 1963), pp. 237–238.

"American View of the Lahti Seminar," *Look at Finland*, 1964, p. 18. [English version of the following entry.]

"Seminariet en succé," *Horisont*, XI (1964), 13–14. [Swedish version of the preceding entry.]

"A Note to the Harvest Edition," *The Misanthrope and Tartuffe*, pp. v–vi [*see above*, A, 2].

"On My Own Work," *Shenandoah*, XVII (Autumn 1965), 57–67; reprinted in *Poets on Poetry*, ed. Howard Nemerov (New York: Basic Books, Inc., 1966), pp. 160–171.

"Poetry and Happiness," *Reflection: The Wesleyan Quarterly*, I (Fall 1966), 13–24 [a speech delivered in Spring 1966 at Wooster College, Wooster, Ohio, at a symposium on "The Arts and the Pursuit of Happiness"]; reprinted in *Shenandoah*, XX (Summer 1969), 3–23 [a lecture delivered on February 20, 1969, in Lexington, Virginia, at the invitation of the Glascow Endowment Committee].

"Introduction" to *Poems, William Shakespeare*, pp. 7–21 [*see above*, A, 3].

"A Poet and the Movies," in *Man and the Movies*, ed. William R. Robinson, with assistance from George Garrett (Baton Rouge: Louisiana State University Press, 1967), pp. 223–226.

"Explaining the Obvious," *New York Times Book Review*, LXXIII (March 17, 1968), 2, 46; reprinted with minor changes as "On 'A Red, Red Rose,' " in *Poetry: An Introduction*, ed. William G. Lane (Boston: D. C. Heath Co., 1968), pp. 353–357.

D. Book reviews

Listed chronologically.

"Between Visits," *Poetry*, LXXIV (May 1949), 114–117. On
C. Day Lewis: *Poems 1943–1947*.

New England Quarterly, XXIII (March 1950), 121–123. On
N. Bryllion Fagan: *The Histrionic Mr. Poe*.

Poetry, LXXVII (November 1950), 105–107. On John
Frederick Nims: *A Fountain in Kentucky and Other Poems*.

"Seven Poets," *Sewanee Review*, LVIII (Winter 1950),
130–143. On William Empson: *Collected Poems of
William Empson*; D. H. Lawrence: *The Selected Poems
of D. H. Lawrence*; William Carlos Williams: *The Selected
Poems of William Carlos Williams*; Elizabeth Daryush:
Selected Poems; John Heath-Stubbs: *The Charity of the
Stars*; Hyam Plutzik: *Aspects of Proteus*; James Broughton:
The Playground.

New England Quarterly, XXIV (March 1951), 125–126. On
William Van O'Connor: *The Shaping Spirit*.

New England Quarterly, XXIV (March 1951), 132. On F. O.
Matthiessen: *The Oxford Book of American Verse*.

"Inclusive View," *Hopkins Review*, V (Fall 1951), 63–65. On
W. H. Auden: *Nones*.

Furioso, VIII (Spring 1953), 57–61. On W. S. Merwin: *A Mask
for Janus*; and Oscar Williams, ed.: *Immortal Poems of
the English Language*.

41

"Robert Graves' New Volume," *Poetry*, LXXXVII (December 1955), 175–179. On *Collected Poems 1955*.

"The Heart of the Thing," *New York Times Book Review*, LXI (November 11, 1956), 18. On Marianne Moore: *Like a Bulwark*.

"And No Place to Call Home," *New York Times Book Review*, LXIV (January 4, 1959), 14. On Yvan Goll: *Jean Sans Terre*.

In "Amherst Authors," *Amherst Alumni News*, January 1959, p. 25. On F. O. Matthiessen: *The Achievement of T. S. Eliot, An Essay on the Nature of Poetry*, with a chapter on Eliot's later work by C. L. Barber.

New York Herald Tribune Book Review, March 25, 1962, p. 3. On Robert Frost: *In the Clearing*.

"Longfellow," *New York Review of Books*, I, Special Issue of Spring & Summer Books (1963), 17. On Newton Arvin: *Longfellow: His Life and Work*.

"The Poe Mystery Case," *New York Review of Books*, IX (July 13, 1967), 16, 25–28. On Eric W. Carlson, ed.: *The Recognition of Edgar Allan Poe: A Collection of Critical Essays*; and Robert Regan, ed.: *Poe: A Collection of Critical Essays*. Wilbur's review prompted a letter to the editor, from Norman N. Holland; it, and Wilbur's reply, were printed in *New York Review of Books*, IX (September 14, 1967).

E. Interviews

Listed chronologically.

"An Interview with Richard Wilbur," ed. David Curry, *Trinity Review*, XVII (December 1962), 21–32.

"Richard Wilbur: An Interview," eds. Robert Frank and Stephen Mitchell, *Amherst Literary Magazine*, X (Summer 1964), 54–72.

"Richard Wilbur Talking to Joan Hutton," ed. Joan Hutton, *Transatlantic Review*, No. 29 (Summer 1968), pp. 58–67.

F. Manuscripts

Most of Richard Wilbur's papers are located at the Robert Frost Library, Amherst College. Additional manuscripts, almost entirely of early work, are in the Poetry Collection, Lockwood Memorial Library, State University of New York at Buffalo.

Lockwood Memorial Library

Holdings consist entirely of poetry. Listed alphabetically. For poems that have been published, the numbers at which citations may be found in section B, 2, above, are included. Each poem is numbered, and quotation marks have been omitted.

1. The Cardinal. Two versions, ink, corrections; fragments; 4 pages.

2. Caserta Garden. One typescript version, corrections; 1 page. No. 25.

3. Castles and Distances. No. 95.

4. Conjuration. One pencil version, corrections; one ink version, corrections; 2 pages. No. 57.

5. The Death of a Toad. One version, ink, corrections; 1 page. No. 54.

6. First Snow in Alsace. One version, pencil, corrections; 2 pages. No. 48.

7. The following day was overcast. . . . One version, pencil, corrections; 1 page.

8. For an American Poet Just Dead. Two versions, ink, corrections; 2 pages. No. 72.

9. For Ellen. One version, pencil, corrections; one fragmentary version; 2 pages. No. 27.

10. Fray Burn Says He Now Intends. One version, pencil, corrections; 1 page.

11. Giacometti. One version, ink, corrections; one fair typescript; 2 pages. No. 80.

12. The Giaour and the Pacha. One version, pencil, corrections; 1 page. No. 28.

13. Grace Falls the Fastest. One typescript version with pencil notations; 1 page. No. 65 ("Lament").

14. Grasse: The Olive Trees. Four versions, ink, corrections; one fair copy; 6 pages. No. 64.

15. Howard Moss. One fair copy.

16. In a city of bad statues. . . . One fair copy; 1 page.

17. [J. M. Brinnin]. One version, pencil, erasure; 1 page.

18. Juggler. Seven versions, pencil, ink, corrections; 9 pages. No 81.

19. Marché aux Oiseaux. One pencil version, corrections; one ink version, correction and alternates; one typescript version, corrections; fragment; 4 pages. No. 86.

20. Nightfalls. Three versions, ink, corrections; one fair typescript; 4 pages. No. 87.

21. The Peace of Cities. One fair copy; 2 pages. No. 35.

22. A Plan for Bondage. One pencil version, corrections; one
    fair copy, pencil; one fair typescript with alternates;
    one fair typescript; one typescript version, corrections;
    5 pages.

23. The plebs. . . . One fair typescript version; 1 page.

24. Returning. Two versions, ink, corrections; one version,
    pencil, corrections; one typescript version, corrections; 4
    pages.

25. Stevens. . . . One fair copy.

26. Still, Citizen Sparrow. One version, ink, corrections; one
    fair typescript; 2 pages. No. 62.

27. Tears for the Rich. One version, pencil, corrections;
    fragments; 4 pages. No. 74.

28. Then When the Ample Season. Two versions, ink, correc-
    tions; one part version; 3 pages. No. 66.

29. Tywater. One pencil version, corrections; 1 page. No. 21.

30. We Are this Man. Two versions, ink, corrections; frag-
    ments; 2 pages.

31. Weather Bird. One pencil version, corrections; two part
    versions, ink; 3 pages. No. 73.

32. Wellfleet: The House. One pencil version, corrections;
    one typescript version, corrections; 2 pages. No. 56.

Robert Frost Library

The Library has issued the following description of its
holdings and their arrangement:
    This collection of Mr. Wilbur's papers is the result
of his continuing generosity in making Amherst

College the repository for his manuscripts. The collection is arranged in four sections: I–Poetry; II–Translations and Adaptations; III–Prose; and IV–Miscellaneous. In the poetry section the materials are divided into two groups—materials used in the publication of Mr. Wilbur's volumes of poetry, and the early worksheets and drafts of individual poems. It is possible to find drafts of the same poem in both groups or in only one of the two groups. Translations of individual poems may be found in both section I, Published Volumes, and section II, Translations of Individual Poems, or in only one of the two groups. The folder for any poem, volume, or article contains the correspondence and other matter relating to that item. The typed notes on the small pieces of paper in many of the folders are Mr. Wilbur's notes which accompanied the material as it was added to the collection.

The list that follows is essentially the same as that provided by the Library. For poems that have been published, the numbers at which citations may be found in section 8, 2, above, are included.

I--Poetry

Box I

Published Volumes (listed chronologically)

Folder

1. *Ceremony*. Worksheets and typescripts for material eliminated from published volume.

2. *Ceremony*. Worksheets and typescripts.

Folder

3. *Ceremony*. Worksheets and typescripts.

4. *Ceremony*. Galley proofs.

5. *Things of This World*. Typescript, setting copy.

6. *Advice to a Prophet*. Worksheets and typescripts.

7. *Advice to a Prophet*. Galley and page proofs.

8. *Walking to Sleep*. Worksheets and typescripts.

9. *Walking to Sleep*. Proofs of front matter, dust jacket, and brochure.

10. *Walking to Sleep*. Proofs of text.

Individual Poems (listed alphabetically)

Folder

11. Advice to a Prophet. No. 156.

12. After the Last Bulletins. No. 121.

13. The Agent. No. 221.

14. Another Voice. No. 157.

15. The Aspen and the Stream. No. 177.

16. Ballade for the Duke of Orléans. No. 167.

17. A Baroque Wall-Fountain in the Villa Sciarra. No text, only Wilbur's commentary. No. 145.

18. The Beacon. No. 114.

—. Beasts. See "Looking into History." No. 110.

19. A Black November Turkey. No. 127.

Folder

20. A Christmas Hymn. No. 180.

21. A Chronic Condition. No. 116.

22. Complaint. No. 195.

23. Digging for China. No. 112.

24. Driftwood. No. 70.

25. Easter Sun ("Parable" was salvaged from this poem).

26. Exeunt (also published as "Exodus"), with drafts of a light poem about the giraffe. No. 115.

27. Fall in Corrales. See also "Speech for the Repeal of the McCarran Act." No. 146.

28. Fern-Beds in Hampshire County. No. 203.

29. A Fire-Truck. No. 154.

30. For Kathleen Raine on her Sixtieth Birthday. No. 212.

31. From the Lookout Rock. No. 67.

32. Gemini. No. 172.

—. Giraffe. See "Exeunt."

33. The Good Servant. No. 103.

34. A Grasshopper. No. 159.

35. He Was. No. 106.

Box II

Individual Poems (continued)

Folder

1. A Hole in the Floor. No. 171.

50

Folder

2. In a Churchyard. No. 216.

3. In the Elegy Season. No. 108.

4. In the Smoking-Car. No. 162.

5. John Chrysostom. No. 139.

6. Junk. No. 178.

7. Lamarck Elaborated (with initial notes for "Mind"). No. 130.

8. A Late Aubade (includes 1968 Christmas card). No. 211.

9. The Lilacs (includes proofs of "The Proof" and "Seed Leaves"). No. 189.

10. Looking into History (includes initial notes for "Beasts," "A Voice from Under the Table," and some unwritten poems). No. 118.

11. Love Calls Us to the Things of This World. No. 141.

12. Loves of the Puppets. No. 150.

13. Matthew VIII, 28 ff. No. 220.

14. The Mechanist. No. 210.

15. Merlin Enthralled. No. 120.

16. The Mill. See also "Speech for the Repeal of the McCarran Act." No. 140.

17. A Miltonic Sonnet for Mr. Johnson, on the occasion of his refusal of Peter Hurd's official portrait. No. 201.

18. Mind. See also "Lamarck Elaborated." No. 132.

19. Next Door. No. 169.

Folder

20. October Maples, Portland. No. 164.

21. On the Marginal Way. No. 196.

—. Parable. See "Easter Sun." No. 92.

—. Piazza di Spagna, Early Morning. See Molière: *Misanthrope*, worksheets. No. 144.

22. A Plain Song for Comadre. No. 131.

23. A Postcard for Bob Bly. No. 207.

24. The Proof (includes page proof for Christmas card). See also "The Lilacs." No. 191.

25. Rillons, Rillettes. No. 197.

26. Running. No. 208.

27. Seed Leaves. See also "The Lilacs." No. 192.

28. Shame. No. 168.

29. She. No. 155.

30. Someone Talking to Himself. No. 153.

31. Speech for the Repeal of the McCarran Act (also notes on "The Mill" and "Fall in Corrales"). No. 109.

32. Stop. No. 166.

33. A Summer Morning. No. 163.

34. The Terrace. No. 83.

35. To Ishtar. No. 173.

36. Two Quatrains for First Frost. No. 160.

37. The Undead. No. 170.

Folder

38. Under Cygnus (includes Christmas card with personal, handwritten note from Mrs. Wilbur). No. 199.

39. A Voice from Under the Table. See also "Looking into History." No. 125.

40. Walking to Sleep. No. 204.

41. A Wood. No. 202.

II--Translations and Adaptations

Translations of Individual Poems (arranged alphabetically by poet)

Folder

42. Akhmatova, Anna. Nos. 174 & 175.

43. Aretino, Pietro.

44. Baudelaire, Charles. Nos. 133–135.

45. Char, René. No. 147.

46. Du Bellay, Joachim. No. 200.

47. Guillén, Jorge. Nos. 158 & 165.

48. Jammes, Francis. No. 124.

49. La Fontaine, Jean de. Nos. 107 & 136.

50. Orléans, Charles, duc d'. No. 193.

51. Pichette, Henri. No. 51.

52. Quasimodo, Salvatore. No. 179.

53. Valéry, Paul. No. 126.

54. Voznesensky, Andrei. Nos. 186, 187, & 198.

Box III

Other Translations

Folder

1. Molière and Hofmannsthal. *The Bourgeois Gentleman*: narration to accompany the Boston Symphony performance of the *Burger als Edelman* by Richard Strauss.

2. Renard, Jules: "A Romance." Corrected typescript.

Molière Translations

Folder

3. *Misanthrope*. Worksheets, mostly Act V (also includes first draft of "Piazza di Spagna, Early Morning").

4. *Misanthrope*. Typescript, setting copy.

5. *Tartuffe*. Worksheets, typescript, and proofs of Introduction and front matter.

6. *Tartuffe*. Worksheets for Act II.

7. *Tartuffe*. Typescript, setting copy.

8. *Tartuffe*. Galley proofs.

9. *Tartuffe*. Worksheets of curtain verses written for opening night.

10. *Tartuffe*. Additional lines for Lincoln Center performance.

11. *Tartuffe*. Notes and drafts for article on the Lincoln Center production.

12. *The Misanthrope and Tartuffe* (Harvest Book Edition). Worksheets and draft of note to the Harvest edition.

13. *The Misanthrope and Tartuffe* (Harvest Book Edition). Proofs of front matter and *Tartuffe*.

III--Prose

Folder

14. *Loudmouse*. Story outline, manuscript, and typescript.

15. *Loudmouse*. Galleys for a new edition.

16. Arvin, Newton: *Longfellow: His Life and Work*. Worksheets for a review.

17. Essay on Milton's companion poems. Worksheets, typescript, and proof.

18. Essay on poetry. Manuscript draft.

19. Frost, Robert: *In the Clearing*. Drafts and typescript of a review.

20. Frost, Robert. Contribution to Robert Frost Commemorative Issue of the *Amherst Student*. Worksheet and typescript.

21. Hillyer, Robert. Draft of a memorial note.

22. Lowell, Robert: "Skunk Hour." Manuscript of commentary.

23. The 1964 International Writers' Seminar at Lahti. Notes, manuscript, and typescript of an article.

24. "The Poe Mystery Case." Manuscript and typescript.

25. "A Poet and the Movies." Worksheets and typescript.

26. *Poems, William Shakespeare*. All matter for an introduction.

Lecture and Speeches

Box IV

Folder

1. Bishop, Elizabeth. Draft and text of introduction to her poetry reading.

Folder

2. Films: manuscript and typescript of a panel talk on experimental films.

3. Frost, Robert. Introduction to his talk.

4. Frost Library, Amherst College. Manuscript and typescript of talk at dedication.

5. "The House of Poe." Manuscript of lecture.

6. Lawrence College, Manuscript, typescript, and printed copy of commencement address.

7. Miller, Henry: *Tropic of Cancer*. Draft of defense testimony.

8. Nash, Ogden. Introduction to his lecture.

9. National Book Award acceptance speech. Drafts and final text.

10. "On My Own Work." Notes, manuscript, and typescript, plus corrected proofs for publication.

11. "Poetry and Happiness." Manuscript of lecture.

12. "The Present State of Whitman." Notes, manuscript, and typescript of talk.

13. Roethke, Theodore. Manuscript and typescript of talk.

14. "Round About a Poem of Housman's." Notes, outline, manuscript, and partial typescript of lecture.

15. "A Tribute to Andrei Voznesensky." Prefatory remarks.

16. Washington University. Notes and typescript of commencement address.

17. Wilbur bibliography. Manuscript and carbon of introductory note [this bibliography, and thus Wilbur's note, have never been published].

IV--Miscellaneous

Folder

18. Light verse on a frog.

19. Answer to questionnaire published in *Delos*.

20. Political activities.

Other Locations

Manuscript collections, 1881–. American Academy of Arts and Letters Library. Correspondence, literary MSS., and other papers. Most of the letters relate to the American Academy of Arts and Letters and to the National Institute of Arts and Letters. Persons represented include Richard Wilbur.

Papers, 1891–1955, of Joseph Warren Beach, Library of Congress, Manuscript Division. Includes correspondence between Beach and Wilbur.

G. Other: Drawings, statements, letter, records, tapes, films

Listed chronologically within sub-categories.

"Common Misconceptions" [drawings], *Touchstone* [Amherst College student magazine], V (March 1940), 9.

Statement in "Statements by Friends and Associates," in memory of F. O. Matthiessen, *Monthly Review*, II (October 1950), 312–313.

"Presentation to Abbie Huston Evans of the Russell Loines Award for Poetry by Richard Wilbur of the Institute," *Proceedings of the American Academy of Arts & Letters and the National Institute of Arts & Letters*, Second Series, No. 11 (New York: Spiral Press, 1961—Publication No. 197), pp. 34–35.

Letter from Richard Wilbur to Paul Cummins, in the unpublished dissertation (University of Southern California, 1967), by Paul Cummins, " 'Difficult Balance': The Poetry of Richard Wilbur," Appendix I, pp. 231–233.

Candide [*see above*, A, 2]. Columbia Records, OS 2350 / OL 5180.

"Love Calls Us to the Things of This World," read by Richard Wilbur, on *The Caedmon Treasury of Modern Poets*. Caedmon Records No. TC 2006 or No. 1067–68.

Twentieth Century Poetry in English. An Album of Modern Poetry, An Anthology Read by the Poets, ed. Oscar Williams. Library of Congress Recording Lab., Washington, D. C. PL 20, 21, 22. Includes a brochure with the full texts of the poems, "Juggler" and "Advice to a Prophet."

Poetry Reading by Richard Wilbur and Stanley Kunitz. New Lecture Hall, Harvard University, July 9, 1959. Boston: Fassett Recording Studio. 2 discs. Lamont Library, Harvard University.

The Poems of Richard Wilbur, Read by the Author. Spoken Arts 747. New Rochelle, N. Y.: Spoken Arts, Inc., 1959. 1 disc. 26 poems.

Many Voices, Album 4 to accompany *Adventures in Appreciation* (grade 10), one of the *Adventures in Literature Series*, Olympic Edition. New York: Harcourt, Brace and Co., 1960.

Richard Wilbur Reading Selections from His Poetry. Morris Gray Lecture, Harvard University, November 21, 1963. Introduction by Professor Reuben Brower. Boston: Fassett Recording Studio. 2 discs. Lamont Library, Harvard University.

Memorial Tribute to Randall Jarrell at Yale University, February 28, 1967, by Robert Lowell, Peter Taylor, Stanley Kunitz, John Hollander, William Meredith, Richard Wilbur, and Mary Jarrell. Boston: Fassett Recording Studio. 2 discs. Lamont Library, Harvard University.

Richard Wilbur Reading His Poetry. Caedmon Treasury TC 1248. New York: Caedmon Records, Inc., 1968. 1 disc. 30 poems.

Richard Wilbur Reading His Own Poems and Translations.
Boston: Transradio Recording. Lamont Library, Harvard
University. 1 disc. 18 poems.

The following recordings are available from the Library of
Congress. See *Literary Recordings,* Library of Congress,
Washington, D. C., 1966, for complete contents and ordering
procedures.

1. *Richard Wilbur.* Reading his poems at Medford, Massachusetts, May 15, 1951. 25 poems, All available on tape
(LWO 1830, reel 3), one on disc (PL 22).

2. *Richard Wilbur.* Reading his poems in the Coolidge Auditorium, Library of Congress, December 2, 1957. 26 poems.
All available on tape (LWO 2609), two on disc (PL 29).

3. *Richard Wilbur.* Reading his poems with commentary in the
Recording Lab., Library of Congress, December 2, 1957.
Includes discussion between Mr. Wilbur and Randall
Jarrell. 7 poems. All available on tape (LWO 2623), two
on disc (PL 29).

4. *Richard Wilbur.* Lecture and reading, "The House of Poe,"
presented in the Coolidge Auditorium, Library of Congress,
November 4, 1959. Tape: LWO 2839.

5. *Richard Wilbur.* Recorded at Yale University, December
1959. Two poems, available on Tape (LWO 2963) or
disc (PL 22).

6. *Johns Hopkins Poetry Festival.* Poets reading their own
poems and the works of others, with commentary, at the
second Johns Hopkins Poetry Festival, October 24–26,
1961. Richard Wilbur reads 12 poems on October 26. All
on tape (LWO 3559), one on disc (PL 29).

7. *National Poetry Festival.* Held in the Coolidge Auditorium,
Library of Congress, October 22–24, 1962. "Introduction of
speakers by Richard Wilbur," October 23 (Tape:
LWO 3869, reel 1). Richard Wilbur reads 4 poems on
October 24 (Tape: LWO 3870, reel 3).

The Poet Speaks. WGBH Radio broadcast, Boston, Massachusetts, February 11, 1952. 2 tapes. 13 poems. Lamont
Library, Harvard University.

*The Cambridge Poets: Richard Wilbur, John Holmes, May
Sarton, Richard Eberhart.* Tape. 6 poems by Wilbur.
Lamont Library, Harvard University.

Untitled tape recording, Lamont Library, Harvard University.
(851.1/4). Richard Wilbur reads 20 poems.

Richard Wilbur, Part I, and *Richard Wilbur,* Part II. Motion
picture produced by the Metropolitan Educational
Television Association, released by National Educational
Television and Radio Center, 1959. Available from Indiana
University, Audio–Visual Center, Bloomington, Indiana
47401, at $6.75 per Part for rental (Catalog Nos.
NET–2184 and NET–2185), or $125 for purchase of both
Parts.

Poetry: Richard Wilbur and Robert Lowell. A 16 mm. motion
picture, 30 minutes, black and white. Interviews Wilbur
and Lowell and explores their interests in poetic expression
and the origins of the ideas in their respective poems.
Wilbur reads three poems. A National Educational Television production, [probably 1967], available from Indiana
University [*see citation above*] at $5.40 for rental
(Catalog No. KS–280).

II. Works about Richard Wilbur
A. Book

Hill, Donald L. *Richard Wilbur*. Twayne's United States
Authors Series. New Haven, Conn.: College & University
Press, 1967. [For a brief review of this book, see Oliver
Evans, "Poetry: The 1930's to the Present," in *American
Literary Scholarship, An Annual, 1967*, ed. James Wood-
ress (Durham, N. C.: Duke University Press, 1969),
p. 274.]

B. Critical articles and commentary in books

Listed alphabetically by author. Anonymous items are
listed chronologically at the end of the author listing.

Abbe, George. *You and Contemporary Poetry*. North Guilford,
Conn.: Author-Audience Publications, 1957, pp. 24–25,
72–80. Reissued: Peterborough, N. H.: Noone House,
1965, pp. 32–33, 98–105. [There are some differences
between the two issues.]

Allen, Don Cameron, ed. *A Celebration of Poets*. Baltimore:
Johns Hopkins University Press, 1967. Originally published, with some differences, as *Four Poets on Poetry*
(1959) and *The Moment of Poetry* (1962), by the same
publisher.

62

Barksdale, Richard K. "Trends in Contemporary Poetry,"
Phylon Quarterly, XIX (Winter 1958), 408–416.

Benedikt, M. "Comment," *Poetry*, CXV (March 1970),
422–425.

Benét, William R. *The Reader's Encyclopedia.* 2nd ed. 2 vols.
New York: Thomas Y. Crowell Co., 1965, II, 1090.

Bly, Robert. "The First Ten Issues of Kayak," *Kayak 12* (1967),
45–49.

Bogan, Louise. *Achievement in American Poetry.* Chicago:
Gateway Editions, Inc., Henry Regnery Co., 1951, pp. 103,
133–134.

Bosquet, Alain, ed. *Trente-Cinq Jeunes Poètes Américans.*
Paris: Gallimard, 1960, "Preface," pp. 9–37; pp 345–352.

Brinnin, John M., and Bill Read, eds. *The Modern Poets, An
American-British Anthology.* New York: McGraw-Hill
Book Co., Inc., 1963, p. 396.

Cambon, Glauco. *Recent American Poetry*, University of Minnesota Pamphlets on American Writers, No. 16.
Minneapolis: University of Minnesota Press, 1962,
pp. 8–16, 42.

Cargill, Oscar. "Poetry Since the Deluge," *English Journal*,
XLIII (February 1954), 57–64.

Clough, Wilson O. "Poe's 'The City in the Sea' Revisited," in
Essays in American Literature in Honor of Jay B. Hubbell,
ed. Clarence Gohdes (Durham, N. C.: Duke University
Press, 1967), pp. 77–89.

Conquest, Robert. "Mistah Eliot—He Dead?" *Audit*, I (March
28, 1960), 12–17.

63

Crowder, Richard. "Richard Wilbur and France," *Rives* (Paris), No. 25 (Spring 1964), pp. 2–8.

Cummins, Paul F. " 'Difficult Balance': The Poetry of Richard Wilbur," unpublished dissertation (University of Southern California, 1967).

————. " 'Difficult Balance': The Poetry of Richard Wilbur," *Dissertation Abstracts*, XXVIII, 3176A.

Curry, David, ed. "An Interview with Richard Wilbur," *Trinity Review*, XVII (December 1962), 21–32.

Daiches, David. "The Anglo-American Difference: Two Views," Part II, in *The Anchor Review*, No. 1, ed Melvin J. Lasky (Garden City, N. Y.: Doubleday & Co., Inc., 1955), pp. 219–233.

Deutsch, Babette. *Poetry in Our Time*. Garden City, N. Y.: Anchor Books / Doubleday & Co., Inc., 1963, pp. 253, 310–311.

Eberhart, Richard. "The Muse—With Yankee Accent," *Saturday Review*, XXXII (March 19, 1949), 8–9, 36.

————. Essay in "On Richard Wilbur's 'Love Calls Us to the Things of This World,' " in Ostroff, pp. 4–5 [*see below*].

Eckman, Frederick. *Cobras and Cockle Shells*: *Modes in Recent Poetry*. Vagrom Chap Book Number Five. New York: The Sparrow Magazine, 1958.

Ehrenpreis, Irvin, Ed. *American Poetry*. Stratford-Upon-Avon Studies 7. London: Edward Arnold Ltd, 1965.

Emerson, Cornelia D. "Books by Richard Wilbur," *Hollins Critic*, VI, Special Issue (July 1969), 7. [A very short bibliography.]

64

Faverty, Frederic E. "Well-Open Eyes; or, the Poetry of Richard Wilbur," *Northwestern University Tri-Quarterly*, II (Fall 1959), 26–30; reprinted in *Poets in Progress*, ed. Edward Hungerford (Evanston, Illinois: Northwestern University Press, 1962 and [with additions] 1967), pp. 59–72 [1967 edition].

Fiedler, Leslie A. "A Kind of Solution: The Situation of Poetry Now." *Kenyon Review*, XXVI (Winter 1964), 54–79.

Field, John P. "The Achievement of Richard Wilbur," unpublished dissertation (University of Cincinnati, 1970).

Flint, R. W. "The Foolproof Style of American Poets," *Audience*, II (November 18, 1955), 1–5.

Foster, Richard. "Debauch by Craft: Problems of the Younger Poets," *Perspective*, XII (Spring–Summer 1960), 3–17.

Frank, Robert, and Stephen Mitchell, eds. "Richard Wilbur: An Interview," *Amherst Literary Magazine*, X (Summer 1964), 54–72 .

Fraser, G. S. "Some Younger American Poets, Art and Reality," *Commentary*, XXIII (May 1957), 454–462.

Fussell, Paul, Jr. *Poetic Meter and Poetic Form.* New York: Random House, 1966, pp. 78–79, 89, 103.

Garrett, George. "Against the Grain, Poets Writing Today," in Ehrenpreis, Chapter X, pp. 220–239 [*see above*].

Geiger, Mary Loretta, Sister. "Structure and Imagery in the Poetry of Richard Wilbur," unpublished master's thesis (Villanova University, 1966).

Greene, George. "Four Campus Poets," *Thought*, XXXV (Summer 1960), 223–246.

Gregory, Horace. "Poetry," Section 3 in "The Postwar Generation in Arts & Letters," ed. Maxwell Geismar, *Saturday Review*, XXXVI (March 14, 1953), 11–19, 64.

Gustafson, Richard. "Richard Wilbur and the Beasts," *Iowa English Yearbook*, No. 11 (Fall 1966), pp. 59–63.

Hall, Donald. "American Poets Since the War," *World Review*, NS 46 (December 1952), pp. 28–32.

————. "American Poets Since the War, II," *World Review*, NS 47 (January 1953), pp. 48–54.

————. "Method in Poetic Composition (with special attention to the techniques of Richard Eberhart and Richard Wilbur)," *Paris Review*, No. 3 (Autumn 1953), pp. 113–119.

————. "The New Poetry: Notes on the Past Fifteen Years in America," in *New World Writing, Seventh Mentor Selection* (New York: New American Library, 1955), pp. 231–247.

————. "Ah, Love, Let Us Be True, Domesticity and History in Contemporary Poetry," *American Scholar*, XXVIII (Summer 1959), 310–319.

————. "The Battle of the Bards," *Horizon*, IV (September 1961), 116–121.

————. "Introduction" to *Contemporary American Poetry*, ed. Donald Hall (Baltimore: Penguin Books, 1962), pp. 17–26.

Harrigan, Anthony. "American Formalists," *South Atlantic Quarterly*, XLIX (October 1950), 483–489.

Hart, James D. *The Oxford Companion to American Literature*. 4th ed. New York: Oxford University Press, 1965, p. 923.

66

Hassan, Ihab. "Since 1945," in *Literary History of the United States*, ed. R. E. Spiller and others, 3rd ed., rev. (New York: Macmillan, 1963), pp. 1430–31.

Hemphill, George. "The Meters of the Intermediate Poets," *Kenyon Review*, XIX (Winter 1957), 37–55.

Hester, Mary, Sister. " 'The Juggler' by Richard Wilbur," *English Journal*, LIV (December 1965), 880–881.

Holmes, John. "Surroundings and Illuminations," in Allen, pp. 108–130 [*see above*].

Horan, Robert. Essay in "On Richard Wilbur's 'Love Calls Us to the Things of This World,' " in Ostroff, pp. 6–11 [*see below*].

Hutton Joan, ed. "Richard Wilbur Talking to Joan Hutton," *Transatlantic Review*, No. 29 (Summer 1968), pp. 58–67.

Jarrell, Randell. "A View of Three Poets," *Partisan Review*, XVIII (November-December 1951), 691–700; reprinted in Jarrell's *Poetry and the Age* (New York: Vintage Books, 1953), as "Three Books," pp. 227–240.

———. "Fifty Years of American Poetry," *Prairie Schooner*, XXXVII (Spring 1963), 1–27.

———. Discussion of Richard Wilbur in *National Poetry Festival* (Washington, D. C.: Library of Congress, 1964), pp. 135–137.

Jerome, Judson. *Poetry: Premeditated Art*. Boston: Houghton Mifflin Co., 1968, pp. 168–169, 179–183, 348–349.

Keith, Joseph J. " 'Giacometti' by Richard Wilbur," *Variegation*, V (Winter 1950), 19.

Kizer, Carolyn. "Poetry of the Fifties: in America," in *International Literary Annual No. 1*, ed. John Wain (London: John Calder, 1958), pp. 60–96. [Includes only a very brief comment on Wilbur.]

Klein, Luce Arthur. "The Poems of Richard Wilbur," commentary on jacket of *The Poems of Richard Wilbur*, Spoken Arts 747 [*see above*, I, G].

Langbaum, Robert. "The New Nature Poetry," *American Scholar*, XXVIII (Summer 1959), 323–340.

McGuinness, Arthur E. "A Question of Consciousness: Richard Wilbur's *Things of This World*," *Arizona Quarterly*, XXIII (Winter 1967), 313–326.

Meredith, William. Commentary on jacket of *Richard Wilbur Reading His Poetry*, Caedmon TC 1248 [*see above*, I, G].

Mills, Ralph J., Jr. *Contemporary American Poetry*. New York: Random House, 1965, pp. 160–175.

Mitchell, Stephen. [*see above*, Frank.]

Monteiro, George. "Redepmtion Through Nature: a Recurring Theme in Thoreau, Frost, and Richard Wilbur," *American Quarterly*, XX (Winter 1968), 795–809.

Myers, John A., Jr. "Death in the Suburbs," *English Journal*, LII (May 1963), 376–379.

Nims, John Frederick. *Poetry: A Critical Supplement*. February 1948, pp. 1–9. [On "Ceremony" and "A Simile for Her Smile."]

————, ed. *A Critical Supplement to Poetry*. December 1948, pp. 1–9. [Explanatory remarks by Wilbur on "Driftwood" and "To an American Poet Just Dead."]

Nyren, Dorothy, ed. *A Library of Literary Criticism*. New York: Frederick Ungar Publishing Co., 1960, pp. 525–527. [Very brief bibliography, of little use.]

Ostroff, Anthony, ed. *The Contemporary Poet as Artist and Critic: Eight Symposia*. Boston: Little, Brown and Co., 1964. The symposium "On Richard Wilbur's 'Love Calls Us to the Things of This World,' " pp. 1–21, was originally published in *Berkeley Review*, I (1957), 31–51.

Plath, Sylvia. "Poets on Campus," *Mademoiselle*, XXXVII (August 1953), 290–291.

Reedy, Gerald, S. J. "The Senses of Richard Wilbur," *Renascence*, XXI (Spring 1969), 145–150.

Ringbom, Mårten, trans. "Richard Wilbur Dikter," *Horisont*, XI (1964), 20–22. [Swedish translation of 4 poems.]

Robinson, James K., and G. W. Allen and W. B. Rideout, eds. *American Poetry*. New York: Harper & Row, 1965, pp. 1240–41.

Rosenthal, M. L. *The Modern Poets: A Critical Introduction*. New York: Oxford University Press, 1960, pp. 8, 248, 253–255.

———. *The New Poets: American and British Poetry Since World War II*. New York: Oxford University Press, 1967, pp. 328–330.

Sarton, May. "The School of Babylon," in Allen, pp. 131–151 [*see above*].

Sayre, Robert F. "A Case for Richard Wilbur as Nature Poet," *Moderna Sprak*, LXI (1967), 114–122.

Schwartz, Joseph, and Robert C. Roby, eds. *Poetry, Meaning and Form*. New York: McGraw-Hill Book Co., 1969, pp. 164–166.

Southworth, James G. "The Poetry of Richard Wilbur," *College English*, XXII (October 1960), 24–29.

Spender, Stephen. "Rhythms That Ring in American Verse, *New York Times Book Review*, LV (September 3, 1950), 3.

Stephanchev, Stephen. *American Poetry Since 1945*. New York: Harper & Row, 1965, pp. 93–106.

Sutton, Walter. "Criticism and Poetry," in Ehrenpreis, Chapter VIII, pp. 174–195 [*see above*].

Swenson, May. Essay in "On Richard Wilbur's 'Love Calls Us to the Things of This World,' " in Ostroff, pp. 12–16 [*see above*].

Taylor, Henry. "Two Worlds Taken As They Come: Richard Wilbur's 'Walking To Sleep,' " *Hollins Critic*, VI, Special Issue (July 1969), 1–12.

Toerien, Barend J. "Verse Van Richard Wilbur," *Tydskrif vir Letterkunde*, XII (June 1962), 13–20. [Article and translations.]

Turnell, Martin. "Introductory Note" to *The Misanthrope*, trans. Richard Wilbur (London: Methuen, 1967) [*see above*, I, A, 2].

Viereck, Peter. "The Last Decade in Poetry: New Dilemmas and New Solutions," in *Literature in the Modern World, Lectures Delivered at George Peabody College for Teachers 1951–1954* (Nashville: Bureau of Publications, George Peabody College for Teachers, 1954), pp. 37–63. The discussion of Wilbur is a slightly revised version of a 1952 review of *Ceremony* [*see below*, C].

Waggoner, Hyatt H. *American Poets: From the Puritans to the Present*. Boston: Houghton Mifflin Co., 1968, pp. 137, 596–604.

Wakefield, Dan. "Night Clubs," *Nation*, CLXXXVI (January 4, 1958), 19–20. [Brief comment.]

Warlow, Francis W. "Richard Wilbur," *Bucknell Review*, VII (May 1958), 217–233.

Weatherhead, A. K. "Richard Wilbur: Poetry of Things," *ELH*, XXXV (December 1968), 606–617.

ANONYMOUS

Times Literary Supplement, LVIII (November 6, 1959), xi–xxxix. Issue on the American Imagination.

"In the Twilight of the Old Order, the Promising New Poets," *National Observer*, April 8, 1963, p. 20.

"Songs Around the Mountain," *Times Literary Supplement*, No. 3326 (November 25, 1965), p. 1070.

C. Book reviews

Listed alphabetically by author, under title of each item
reviewed in chronological order of publication or
presentation. Anonymous reviews are listed chronologically
at the end of each sub-section.

1. *The Beautiful Changes*

Bogan, Louise. "Verse," *New Yorker*, XXIII (November 15,
1947), 133–134.

Cole, Thomas. "Poetry and Painting: The Poetry of Richard
Wilbur," *Imagi*, IV (Winter 1949), 11–12.

Daiches, David. "Right and Wrong Tracks," *Saturday Review*,
XXXI (January 10, 1948), 17.

Deutsch, Babette. *Tomorrow*, VIII (October 1948), 58–59.

Eberhart, Richard. "Jewels of Rhythm," *New York Times Book
Review*, LIII (January 11, 1948), 4.

Fitzgerald, Robert. *New Republic*, CXXI (August 8, 1949), 18.

Golffing, F. C. "A Remarkable New Talent," *Poetry*, LXXI
(January 1948), 221–223.

Heringman, Bernard. "A Talent Definitely Worth Considera-
tion," *Imagi*, IV (1948), 13–14.

Kennedy, Leo. *Chicago Sun Book Week*, December 3, 1947,
p. 8A.

Knight, Douglas M. "New Verse," *Furioso*, III (Winter 1947), 61–64.

Rosenthal, M. L. "Speak the Whole Mind," *New York Herald Tribune Book Review*, March 21, 1948, p. 8.

Strachan, Pearl. "Poet's Eye," *Christian Science Monitor*, November 29, 1947, p. 17.

Swallow, Alan. "Some Current Poetry," *New Mexico Quarterly*, XVIII (Winter 1948), 455–462.

ANONYMOUS

Kirkus, XV (October 15, 1947), 594.

2. *Ceremony*

Bennett, Joseph. "Five Books, Four Poets," *Hudson Review*, IV (Spring 1951), 133–143.

Bogan, Louise. "Verse," *New Yorker*, XXVII (June 9, 1951), 109-133.

Cahoon, Herbert. *Library Journal*, LXXVI (January 1, 1951), 49.

Cole, Thomas. "Poetry and Its Phases," *Voices*, No. 145 (May–August 1951), pp. 37–41.

———. "Wilbur's Second Volume," *Poetry*, LXXXII (April 1953), 37–39.

Daiches, David. "Uncommon Poetic Gift," *New York Herald Tribune Book Review*, XXVII (February 18, 1951), 4.

Deutsch, Babette. "Scenes Alive with Light," *New York Times Book Review*, LVI (February 11, 1951), 12.

Humphries, Rolfe. "Verse Chronicle," *Nation*, CLXXI (December 9, 1950), 535–536.

Nims, John Frederick. *Chicago Sunday Tribune Magazine of Books*, March 11, 1951, p. 2.

Vazakas, Byron. "Eleven Contemporary Poets," *New Mexico Quarterly*, XXII (Summer 1952), 213–229.

Viereck, Peter. "Technique and Inspiration, A Year of Poetry," *Atlantic*, CLXXXIX (January 1952), 81–83. This review was slightly revised and delivered in a speech in 1954 [*see above*, B].

West, Ray B., Jr. "The Tiger in the Wood: Five Contemporary Poets," *Western Review*, XVI (Autumn 1951), 76–84.

Whittmore, Reed. "Verses," *Furioso*, VI (Spring 1951), 80–82.

ANONYMOUS

Kirkus, XVIII (November 15, 1950), 690.

United States Quarterly Book Review, VII (March 1951), 28.

Cleveland Open Shelf, March 1951, p. 5.

Booklist, XLVII (April 15, 1951), 291.

3. *A Bestiary*

Ciardi, John. "Our Most Melodic Poet," *Saturday Review*, XXXIX (August 18, 1956), 18–19.

4. *The Misanthrope*

Many of the reviews of *The Misanthrope* have been collected and reprinted in *New York Theatre Critics Reviews 1968* (New York: Critics Theatre Reviews, Inc., 1969), pp. 216–218; cited below as *TCR*.

74

Barnes, Clive. "The Theatre: A Timely 'Misanthrope,' " *New York Times*, October 10, 1968; in *TCR*, pp. 216–217.

Becker, William. "Some French Plays in Translation," *Hudson Review*, IX (Summer 1956), 277–288.

Chapman, John. " 'Misanthrope' Sparkles at APA," *Daily News*, October 10, 1968; in *TCR*, p. 216.

Ciardi, John. "Our Most Melodic Poet," *Saturday Review*, XXXIX (August 18, 1956), 18–19.

Clurman, Harold. *Nation*, CCVII (November 11, 1968), 510.

Cooke, Richard P. "Rebounding with Moliere," *Wall Street Journal*, October 11, 1968; in *TCR*, p. 218.

Gill, Brendan. "Poets and Others," *New Yorker*, XLIV (October 19, 1968), 159–160.

Gottfried, Martin. " 'The Misanthrope,' " *Women's Wear Daily*, October 10, 1968; in *TCR*, p. 218.

Hall, Donald. "Claims on the Poet," *Poetry*, LXXXVIII (September 1956), 398–403.

Harris, Leonard. "*Misanthrope*," *WCBS TV2*, October 9, 1968; in *TCR*, p. 218.

Hewes, Henry. "The Theatre," *Saturday Review*, LI (November 2, 1968), 53.

Park, Bruce R. "Some Versions of Drama," *Accent*, XVI (Winter 1956), 67–70.

Probst, Leonard. "*The Misanthrope*," *NBC 4TV*, October 9, 1968; in *TCR*, p. 218.

Reilly, John H. "Timeless and Timely," *Christian Century*, LXXXV (November 27, 1968), 1509–10.

Watts, Richard, Jr. "Moliere in the Best of Hands," *New York Post*, October 10, 1968; in *TCR*, p. 217.

West, Anthony. "*The Misanthrope*, 'faultlessly,' " *Vogue*, CLIII (January 1, 1969), 70.

ANONYMOUS

Year's Work in English Studies, 1958, p. 39.
America, CXIX (November 9, 1968), 445–447.

5. *Things of This World*

Ashman, Richard. *Talisman 10* (Winter 1956 / Spring 1957), 61–69.

Bogan, Louise. "Verse," *New Yorker*, XXXII (October 6, 1956), 178–181.

Bogardus, Edgar. "The Flights of Love," *Kenyon Review*, XIX (Winter 1957), 137–144.

Ciardi, John. "Our Most Melodic Poet," *Saturday Review*, XXXIX (August 18, 1956), 18–19.

Deutsch, Babette. "The Grace and Wit of a 'Poet's Poet,' " *New York Herald Tribune Book Review*, July 8, 1956, p. 2.

Drake, Leah B. "New Voices in Poetry," *Atlantic*, CXCIX (June 1957), 75–78.

Eberhart, Richard. "Strong, Sensitive and Balanced," *New York Times Book Review*, LXI (June 24, 1956), 5.

Engle, Paul. "Brilliant Pages," *Chicago Sunday Tribune Magazine of Books*, September 16, 1956, p. 4.

Ghiselin, Brewster. "The Best of Richard Wilbur," *Poetry Broadside*, I (Summer 1957), 11, 14.

Gibbs, Alonzo. "Four Abreast," *Voices*, No. 163 (May–August 1957), pp. 43–46.

Gregory, Horace. "The Poetry of Suburbia," *Partisan Review*, XXIII (Fall 1956), 545–553.

Hall, Donald. "Claims on the Poet," *Poetry*, LXXXVIII (September 1956), 398–403.

Hecht, Anthony. "Poetry Chronicle," *Hudson Review*, IX (Autumn 1956), 444–457.

Langland, Joseph. "A Contrast of Excellence," *Northwest Review*, I (Spring 1957), 56–60.

Logan, John. "To the Silly Eye," *Commonweal*, LXIV (August 10, 1956), 474.

McDonald, G. D. *Library Journal*, LXXXI (October 1, 1956), 2262.

Nordell, Rod. *Christian Science Monitor*, June 28, 1956, p. 11.

Plutzik, Hyam. "Recent Poetry," *Yale Review*, NS, XLVI (December 1956), 295–296.

Rosenthal, M. L. "Tradition and Transition," *Nation*, CLXXXIII (November 3, 1956), 372–374.

Scott, Nathan A., Jr. "Literalist of the Imagination," *Christian Century*, LXXV (March 19, 1958), 344–345.

Tobin, James E. "The World and Beyond," *Spirit*, XXIII (January 1957), 189–191.

ANONYMOUS

Booklist, LIII (September 1, 1956), 16.

6. *Candide*

Many of the reviews of *Candide* have been collected and reprinted in *New York Theatre Critics Reviews* 1956 (New York: Critics Theatre Reviews, Inc., 1957), pp. 176–179; cited below as *TCR*.

Atkinson, Brooks. "Musical 'Candide,' " *New York Times*, CVI (December 9, 1956), Section 2, p. X5.

Chapman, John. " 'Candide' an Artistic Triumph; Bernstein's Score Magnificent," *Daily News*, December 3, 1956; in *TCR*, p. 176.

Coleman, Robert. "Musical 'Candide' Is Distinguished Work," *Daily-Mirror*, December 3, 1956; in *TCR*, p. 179.

Donnelly, Tom. "Best Musical News of Year is Found in New 'Candide,' " *New York World-Telegram and The Sun*, December 3, 1956; in *TCR*, p. 177.

Gibbs, Walcott. "Voltaire Today," *New Yorker*, XXXII (December 15, 1956), 52–54.

Hobson, Laura Z. "Trade Winds," *Saturday Review*, XXXIX (September 8, 1956), 10, 12.

Kerr, Walter. " 'Candide,' " *New York Herald Tribune*, December 3, 1956; in *TCR*, p. 179.

McClain, John. "Fine, Bright—But Operetta Lacks Spark," *Journal-American*, December 3, 1956; in *TCR*, p. 178.

Watts, Richard, Jr. "Voltaire's 'Candide' as an Operetta," *New York Post*, December 3, 1956; in *TCR*, p. 178.

7. *Poems 1943–1956*

Asselineau, Roger. "Les Fleurs de Verre de Richard Wilbur," *Critique* (Paris), XVI (October 1960), 844–848.

Fraser, G. S. "Parnassian Grades," *New Statesman and Nation,* NS, LIII (May 18, 1957), 649–650.

Lerner, L. D. "Baroque Rationalist," *Listen,* II (Summer–Autumn 1957), 23–26.

ANONYMOUS

"Modern Wit-Poet," *Times Literary Supplement,* No. 2281 (May 17, 1957), p. 306.

8.   *Advice to a Prophet*

Abse, Dannie. "Variety and Obsession," *Poetry Review,* NS, LIV (Spring 1963), 108–110.

Derrick, Christopher, "Power and Laws," *Tablet* (London), CCXVII (February 16, 1963), 169–170.

Deutsch, Babette. "Seasonal Miracles and Permanent Truths," *New York Herald Tribune Book Review,* December 3, 1961, p. 4.

Dickey, James. "The Stillness at the Center of the Target," *Sewanee Review,* LXX (Summer 1962), 484–504; the section on Wilbur is reprinted in Dickey's *Babel to Byzantium, Poets & Poetry Now* (New York: Farrar, Straus & Giroux, 1968), pp. 170–172.

Dickinson, Peter. *Punch,* CCXLIV (January 2, 1963), 31.

Enright, D. J. "The Greater Toil," *New Statesman,* LXV (January 4, 1963), 21–22.

Fitts, Dudley. "A Trio of Singers in Varied Keys," *New York Times Book Review,* LX (October 29, 1961), 16.

Flint, R. W. "The Road From Rome" *Partisan Review,* XXIX (Winter 1962), 147–148.

Furbank, P. N. "New Poetry," *Listner* (London), LXIX (March 7, 1963), 435.

Gunn, Thom. "Imitations and Originals," *Yale Review*, NS, LI (March 1962), 482.

Hazo, Samuel. "A Clutch of Poets," *Commonweal*, LXXV (December 22, 1961), 346.

Holmes, John. *Christian Science Monitor*, December 21, 1961, p. 7.

Holmes, Theodore. "A Prophet Without A Prophecy," Part I of Wilbur's New Book: Two Views," *Poetry*, C (April 1962), 37–39 [*see below*, Meredith].

Kell, Richard. *Critical Quarterly* (London), V (Autumn 1963), 283–284.

Meredith, William. "A Note on Richard Wilbur," Part II of "Wilbur's New Book: Two Views," *Poetry*, C (April 1962), 40 [*see above*, Theodore Holmes].

Mills, Ralph J., Jr. "The Lyricism of Richard Wilbur," *Modern Age*, VI (Fall 1962), 436–440.

Morse, Samuel F. *Virginia Quarterly Review*, XXXVIII (Spring 1962), 324–330.

O'Connor, William Van. "The Recent Contours of the Muse," *Saturday Review*, XLV (January 9, 1962), 68–71.

Osborne, Charles. "Among the Poetmen," *Spectator* (London) CCIX (December 21, 1962), 969.

Philbrick, Charles. *Mutiny 12* (1963), 62–63.

Press, John. *The Sunday Times* (London).

Pugh, Griffith T. "From the Recent Books," *English Journal*, LI (May 1962), 375.

Robie, Burton A. *Library Journal*, LXXXVI (December 1, 1961), 4192.

Rosenthal, M. L. "An Unfair Question," *Reporter*, XXVI (February 15, 1962), 48–51.

Schevill, James. *San Francisco Sunday Chronicle, This World Magazine*, XXV (December 3, 1961), 31.

Simon, John. "More Brass Than Enduring," *Hudson Review*, XV (Autumn 1962), 455–468.

Stepanchev, Stephen. "In Praise of Craft," *Spirit* (New York), XXVIII (January 1962), 163–165.

Whittmore, Reed. "Packing Up for Devil's Island," *Kenyon Review* XXIV (Spring 1962), 372–377.

ANONYMOUS

Kirkus, XXIX (September 1, 1961), 824.

Christian Century, LXXIX (May 16, 1962), 631.

Bookmark, XXI (June 1962), 258.

"Cowboys and Indians," *Times Literary Supplement*, No. 3177 (January 18, 1963), p. 42; reprinted in *T.L.S., Essays and Reviews from the Times Literary Supplement*, 1963, II (London: Oxford University Press, 1964), pp. 133–136.

"Contemporary Poets Who Deserve a Reading," *The Sunday Times* (London), March 14, 1963, p. 17.

9. *Tartuffe*

Many of the reviews of *Tartuffe* have been collected and reprinted in *New York Theatre Critics Reviews 1965* (New York: Critics Theatre Reviews, Inc., 1966), pp. 390–393; cited below as *TCR*.

Brustein, Robert. "Health in an Ailing Profession," *New Republic*, CLII (January 20, 1965), 32–35.

Chapman, John. " 'Tartuffe' a Rollicking Big Romp; Best Yet for Lincoln Center Co.," *Daily News*, January 15, 1965; in *TCR*, p. 393.

Coke, J. W. "Et Tartuffe?" *Minnesota Review*, V (January–April 1965), 79–83.

Freedley, George. *Library Journal*, LXXXVIII (October 15, 1963), 3859.

Hewes, Henry. "Broadway Postcript," *Saturday Review*, XLVIII (February 6, 1965), 44.

Kerr, Walter. *New York Herald Tribune*, January 16, 1965; in *TCR*, p. 392.

Lerner, Laurence. "Molière's *Tartuffe*," *Listener* (London), LXXI (May 14, 1964), 809.

Lewis, Theophilus. "Theatre," *America*, CXII (March 6, 1965), 336.

McClain, John. " 'Tartuffe'—Lincoln Center Repertory," *New York Journal-American*, January 15, 1965; in *TCR*, p. 390.

Matthews, Jackson. "A New Tartuffe," *New York Review of Books*, I (September 26, 1963), 19–20.

Mercier, Vivian. "No Second Miracle," *Hudson Review*, XVI (Winter 1963–64), 634–636.

Morris. Ivan. "*Tartuffe*, 'grotesquely overacted,' " *Vogue*, CXLV (March 1, 1965), 95.

Nadel, Norman. "Five Words From Tartuffe, and 'Tartuffe' is Saved," *New York World-Telegram and The Sun*, January 15, 1965; in *TCR*, pp. 391–392.

Novick, Julius. "Tartuffe," *Nation*, CC (February 1, 1965), 122.

Sheed, Wilfrid. "The Comedy of Quaintness," *Commonweal*, LXXXI (February 5, 1965), 611–612.

Taubman, Howard. "The Theatre: 'Tartuffe,' " *New York Times*, January 15, 1965; in *TCR*, pp. 390–391.

Watts, Richard, Jr. "Notable Production of 'Tartuffe,' " *New York Post*, January 15, 1965; in *TCR*, p. 393.

ANONYMOUS

"Molière Then and Now," *Times Literary Supplement*, LXIII (April 23, 1964), 336.

Virginia Quarterly Review, XL (Winter 1964), xxv-xxvi.

Variety, January 20, 1965.

"A God of Common Sense," *Time*, LXXXV (January 22, 1965), 46.

"Happy Hypocrite," *Newsweek*, LXV (January 25, 1965), 86.

10. *The Poems of Richard Wilbur*

Gullans, Charles. "Edgar Bowers' *The Astronomers*, and Other New Verse," *Southern Review*, NS, II (Winter 1966), 189–209.

Wallace, Robert M. "Second Impressions, Review of Paperbacks," *Nation*, CXCVII (December 28, 1963), 463.

11. *Loudmouse*

Anonymous. *Kirkus*, XXXVI (January 15, 1968), 50.

12. *Walking to Sleep*

Dickey, William. "A Place in the Country," *Hudson Review*, XXII (Summer 1969), 347–364.

Howes, Victor. *Christian Science Monitor*, 1969.

Kramer, Aaron. *Library Journal*, XCIV (April 15, 1969), 1639.

Mills, Ralph J., Jr. *Chicago Sun-Times, Book Week*, 1969.

Pritchard, William H. In "Amherst Authors," *Amherst Alumni News*, XXII (Summer 1969), 36.

Ratti, John. "Poets in Contrast," *New Leader*, LII (June 9, 1969), 25–26.

Schott, Webster. "A Poet with the Strength of a Genie," *Life*, LXVI, New England Regional Issue (March 14, 1969).

Walsh, Chad. "Contemporary Poetry: Variety Is Its Vitality," *Book World*, III (July 27, 1969), 7.

Williams, Miller. "More Than Jewelry and Crystal," *Saturday Review*, LII (June 14, 1969), 32–34.

13. Other

Kunitz, Stanley. "Poems Recorded by Richard Wilbur," *Evergreen Review*, II (Spring 1959), 201–202. On *The Poems of Richard Wilbur*, Spoken Arts 747 [*see above*, I, G].

Schott, Webster. "Plain Vanilla," *Prairie Schooner*, XXXVI (Spring 1962), 88–90. On *Poets at Wesleyan* [*see above*, I, B, 2, No. 163].

D. Biography

Listed chronologically.

Kunitz, Stanley, ed. *Twentieth Century Authors*, First Supplement. New York: H. W. Wilson Co., 1955, pp. 1079–80.

Smith, John J., ed. *Americana Annual 1958*. New York: Americana Corp., 1958, p. 833.

Handley-Taylor, G., ed. *The International Who's Who in Poetry*, II. London: Cranbrook Tower Press, 1958, p. 152.

Kopkind, Arthur. *Washington Post Books*, May 5, 1959, p. 8.

Anonymous. *New York Herald Tribune Book Review*, March 25, 1962, p. 3.

Untermeyer, Louis, ed. *Modern American Poetry*. New York: Harcourt, Brace & World, Inc., 1962, pp. 673–674.

Anonymous. "Biographical Sketch," in *Poetry in Crystal*, pp. 82–83 [*see above*, I, B, 2, No. 185].

Spender, Stephen, and Donald Hall, eds. *The Concise Encyclopedia of English and American Poets and Poetry*. New York: Hawthorn Books Inc., 1963, p. 357.

The National Cyclopaedia of American Biography, Vol. J (1960–63). New York: James T. White & Co., 1964, 314–315.

Moritz, Charles, ed. *Current Biography 1966*. New York: H. W. Wilson Co., 1966, pp. 440–442.

Contemporary Authors, I–IV. 1st rev. Detroit: Gale Research Co., 1967, p. 1002.

Literary and Library Prizes, 6th ed., rev. and enlarged by Olga S. Weber. New York & London: R. R. Bowker Co., 1967, pp. 13, 67, 101, 124, 207, 210, 211, 214, 216, 219.

Robinson, William R., ed. *Man and the Movies*. Baton Rouge: Louisiana State University Press, 1967, p. 364.

International Who's Who 1968–69, 32nd ed. London: Europa Publications Ltd., 1968, p. 1416.

Who's Who in America, XXXV (1968-69). Chicago: Marquis-Who's Who Inc., 1968, pp. 2347–48.

Muir, Willa. *Belonging, A Memoir*. London: The Hogarth Press, 1968, pp. 291, 294, 297, 299.

Anonymous. "Richard Purdy Wilbur," *Hollins Critic*, VI, Special Issue (July 1969), 5.

Directory of American Scholars, II: English, Speech and Drama. 5th ed. New York: Jaques Cattell Press, 1969, p. 581.